To Semir —
A fellow seeker.
Thanks for your
interest!

— Joe

LETTERS FROM THE
OTHER SIDE OF SILENCE

J
O
S
E
P
H

L
I
T
T
L
E

LETTERS FROM THE OTHER SIDE OF SILENCE

Homebound Publications
Ensuring that the mainstream isn't the only stream.

HOMEBOUND PUBLICATIONS
Ensuring the mainstream isn't the only stream.

Copyright © 2017 by Joseph Little
All Rights Reserved
Printed in the United States of America,
United Kingdom, and Australia.
First Edition Trade Paperback, 2016

Paperback ISBN 978-1-938846-95-3

Front Cover and Interior Image © Elina Li | Shutterstock.com
Cover and Interior Designed by Leslie M. Browning

www.homeboundpublications.com

10 9 8 7 6 5 4 3 2 1

Homebound Publications greatly values the natural environment
and invests in environmental conservation. Our books are printed
on paper with chain of custody certification from the Forest
stewardship Council, Sustainable Forestry Initiative, and the Program
for the Endorsement of Forest Certification. In addition, each
year Homebound Publications donates 1% of our net profit to a
humanitarian or ecological charity.

All author profits from the sale of this book will be donated to the Friendship Village, a home, school, and clinic in Hanoi, Vietnam, for approximately 120 children and young adults living with disability owing to exposure to Agent Orange.

～

To the lamplighters

Steve

Robert

Samantha

Balrum

Belden

Mom

Yuri

HERE'S THE TRUTH: Something happened on that volcano in Guatemala. I'm just not sure what.

Steve was in the lead, talking with two teachers from Canada. I was trailing behind, nursing a bad knee. Yes, Steve was in the lead and I was trailing behind and then it happened.

The volcano in question was Pacaya, that black monster of the western highlands known for its dramatic displays of lava, which surge against prediction and against a landscape so austere it rivals the moon. We found Pacaya in Steve's guidebook one Easter weekend. Something about punishing switchbacks and menacing rivers of lava over which folks could roast marshmallows (and they did), and we were in. It all seemed so sensible from the sturdy haven of our friend's summer cottage, Merlot in hand.

Somewhere around 8,000 feet, that all changed. The lush trees that lined our path gave way to shards of basalt, then rock, then long slopes of rubble that climbed into the sky. What few trees remained were arthritic and bent, their charred branches calli‧graphic against the bright Mayan sky. Soon there was no path, only a windswept ascent that stratified everyone by ability. We would turn a corner, and strange new vistas would appear: jagged fissures in the earth two yards long, coils of braided rock, and waves, waves of lava having long been cooled, blackened, their motion frozen in time. "Pahoehoes," they call them, these cases of rock becoming liquid becoming solid again. Stray dogs in need of warmth sought the company of the fissures, natural manhole covers that vented sulphur and steam from beneath the earth's crust.

After our final turn, I felt the heat of the lava a few seconds before I saw it. After an hour's hike, it was more than a little disappointing—a small vein of red oozing from a titanic wall of black rock (punishing switchbacks, yes, but a river of hellfire this was not)—until I witnessed the wall itself swell and glow, breathing in ways my Midwestern eyes couldn't reckon. At first, I thought it was just the heat shimmering off the wall, the way a paved road can make the summer horizon dance, but then it cracked. Cracked, I tell you, after centuries, maybe millennia of indifference to the world. The wall cracked and began to crumble, spewing impermanence everywhere as it dismantled itself boulder by fiery boulder until nothing remained but a sea of orange suede.

It was too much for me, all that cracking and dismantling. Nearby noises, Steve's banter with the Canadians, the guide's "*vamos! vamos!*": It all retreated into the distance. And then, with no warning, it happened: My syntax simply departed, leaving my words to float in the atmosphere like dust. My rationality, drifting out there among the birds. Soon enough, the words themselves scattered and dissolved, leaving me to experience the world without categories, without reference. Ever tried to take a math test while falling into a lake while sleeping? Well, it was just like that.

I know what you're thinking. No, I wasn't high up there on Pacaya. I wasn't low. I wasn't looking for an experience to transform my life into something special. Stripped of language, I simply slipped beneath it all—and by it all, I suppose I mean my mind—to a place where even fundamental distinctions were no longer clear, like the difference between you and me, right from left, now and not-now. And though mighty and positive, it was also a place of purgation, an evisceration of the psyche, you might say. Truth be told, I want to use the word cosmic here because cosmic it was: an encounter with a God mysterious, though not the God of Michelangelo's making, not ol' Greybeard from my youth. No, it was an imageless God up there on that mountain, a cosmic Whole, an intimate presence that made all things One.

I don't remember the hike down or much of the flight home, but when I got there, I threw out 30 books I knew I'd never read. I've since thrown out 30 more. I took art off my walls. I cut my hair. I trimmed my fingernails and cleaned my car. I cancelled Netflix. I no longer enjoy martinis. Let me say that again: I no longer enjoy martinis. I focus more on people and less on my perception of their perception of me. I used to think the circle was the perfect form. Now I only like circles when I imagine them collapsing on themselves, realizing their ultimate point form. If a circle's just going to hang around being a circle, it's wasting space I figure. The world doesn't need another lazy abstraction.

Where, I ask you, where will this profound sense of economy lead? All I can come up with is "my vanishing, my vanishing." That's what I'd say if I were a betting man.

THE PAST SEVERAL MONTHS have been one long string of Hallelujahs. Having kicked the martinis, the books, the Netflix to the curb, I found a life lean and kinetic, pulsating like the body of a teenager. And the world, it now bulges with significance: Every tree branch bows under the weight of some unutterable wisdom. Every drop of water seems ripe with creation.

The air has a kind of electricity to it, and time itself jerks along in discrete units. There are days when I swear I can sense the universe reconstituting itself moment by moment, like a film or a TV screen: individual pulses too fast for the eye to perceive. The quanta are real, I say to myself, time's apparent continuity, the illusion.

Recently, I've turned to poetry to try to express these holy moments. It's not particularly good poetry, mind you, but what is astonishing to me is the ease with which they write themselves into existence. They come to me in the car, on the street, in the shower. They come to me fully formed as if someone else wrote them. This summer, a few came to me while I was resting in a hotel garden in Poland (I was visiting my grandfather's birthplace, Szeroki Kamien, and got delayed by the floods). It was as if I'd opened my mouth and butterflies flew out. I wrote them down and sent them off to *The Antigonish Review*. We'll see what comes of that.

In private conversations, I've been catching myself using phrases like "The Great Unnameable" and "The Cosmos" instead of the "God" and "Heaven" of my upbringing. And in my journal writing, I pour onto scraps of paper words at once mysterious and oddly familiar, like:

What am I? I am aware of myself as a resilient bubble deep in the sea, confident I will be reunited with the Atmosphere from which I was separated so long ago.

A deeper spiritual life. What does that mean? Deeper into ourselves? Deeper as a more intense emotion? Deeper into the marrow of others?

On the leading edge of the mind, only crusts of words remain.

Sweetness, then darkness. For every A-B, there is a B-A that follows.

What is this palindromic nature that light and heat record?

That I might wince and wonder, of might and much discord, me or my evil twin, pecking away at my soul, a buzzard within.

Raises me to reverie
Rapids of the mind, left behind
Divining the skies
Scratching the wind
You are to me as sun to snow.

There's a difference between (1) the idea of growing old together and (2) growing old together. The second one is truer; the first, an expectation, a mental construct, an artifice. It impedes the flow of reality, places a cracked window between you and existence. There is a peril to conceptual living.

I browse magazines and all I see are abstractions, concepts bereft of a pulse: Christian, Republican, obesity, shamanism, fascism, Buddhism, modernism. I think to myself, I've never met an -ism. I scour the language but find only words that stand in for whole families of experiences, moments of the human condition so cleaned and shaven by the sharp edges of thought that I'm sure something important has been lost. I slowly focus on the moment, I slowly get beyond the words, beyond the analytic categories, beyond the paper, and I descend into silence. That's when I come alive.

I can sneak up on my mind, startle it, separate its stream of consciousness from a faint but growing awareness of reality "out there." I can see my obsessiveness, my worry, my personality, as distinct from the true nature and dangers and delights of the world. And it gives me peace.

I'm also more aware of my emotions these days, and less likely to be held captive by them. I can see that they are conjured by my mind, and, like the weather, they tend to breeze by in time. It's not that they're unimportant—my emotions, my thoughts—but they're not the totality of me. They are like the atmosphere, and there is something to me akin to the earth.

There are days when I refuse to use language at all to refer to the divine out of the growing conviction that all language—even a symbol like a circle or a cross—is inadequate for such a purpose, a slap in the face of the Great Unnameable, though even here I have to remind myself that there's no face to slap, yet another example of language's folly. The divine is perfect, language is not, to use the latter as a substitute for the former is therefore ill conceived. Isn't it? This seems to be the simple logic that clothes the naked impulse emanating from me, but it's the impulse and not the logic that motivates my silence, an impulse whose origin I can trace precisely to Pacaya, when that wall of rock dismantled itself at 8,000 feet and in so doing dismantled me, an impulse which over time has taught me to think in plain truths and then not to think at all.

Back home, on the shores of Lake Ontario, I sit and chant to the beating of an inner rhythm and stir and tremble and, Hallelujah, spill out into the universe over and over again. It's my finest form of prayer.

THERE'S A PART OF ME THAT'S CONTENT to simply delight in the mystery of life: to write poems and prose about Pacaya, to spend good time with family and friends, to immerse myself in wordless trance down by the lake. But there's another part of me that desires understanding. It isn't enough to be dazzled by existence anymore. I want to understand that existence, harness it in some way, extend and expand and improve upon it. I don't want to squander this opportunity to grow in my conscious control of these mystical experiences. I was crossing into Canada the other day and noticed a Lyndon B. Johnson quote in my passport: "For this is what America is all about. It is the uncrossed desert and the unclimbed ridge. It is the star that is not reached and the harvest sleeping in the unplowed ground. . . . Is a new world coming? We welcome it—and we will bend it to the hopes of man." I'm embarrassed to say this, but there's a little LBJ in me.

So, a few months ago, I began what you might call a homemade education. Into the Google machine went words that clumsily described my experience on Pacaya, and out came books like William James' *Varieties of Religious Experience*, William Johnston's *Christian Zen*, and Belden Lane's *The Solace of Fierce Landscapes*. Out poured images too: the Japanese enso, the Celtic cross, and dramatic mountain landscapes the world over. After a few clicks on Amazon and a walk to the mailbox, the journey began.

It was in James' *Varieties* that I first came across the word mysticism. Writing in 1901, James realized it would be impossible to precisely define such an elusive term, so instead he proposed four signs of its presence.

Mystical experiences, I learned, are ineffable. Like love and profound loss, they cannot be adequately described in words. They can be truly felt, truly lived, but they can never be truly under-stood—if by understanding we mean they are capable of being grasped by thought. Here, right here, is the problem of the Great Unnameable, James giving it the name "ineffability," this problem of the inability of language to adequately symbolize what means most to us in this world. This overflowing of the experience of life beyond the bounds of rational discourse: It's become all too famil-iar to me in the year and a half since Pacaya. Even now, depending on which day of the week you ask me, I'll refer to what happened on that mountain as "a little death," a "communion," a "something less than nothing," "an encounter with a place beyond silence," or simply "the elsewhere," and yet even as I speak these words, I can feel their inadequacy building. It's strange: It's not that I'm traf-ficking in falsehoods, but I'm not able to tell the exact truth either. When it really comes down to it, does language make half-liars out of all of us?

Mystical experiences also have what James called a "noetic quality." Although intense emotions are never far behind, folks who have mystical experiences are confident they are encountering deep and abiding truths about the nature of reality. They're not just insights, but "illuminations, revelations, full of significance and importance," wrote James, "all inarticulate though they remain; and as a rule they carry with them a curious sense of authority for after-time." For me, it wasn't just an intense emotional experience like ecstasy or euphoria, nor was it strictly a noetic moment of peering into the heart of some ineffable truth, though that was certainly an important part of it. While reading James, I came to understand Pacaya as an experience of a third kind: part feeling, part knowing, but first something else—a moment of absolute nothingness somehow combined with an awareness of the oneness of all things, an awareness too deep for thought, too deep even for tears, but one that manages to swim along the floor of my consciousness still today. Only after that initial moment of awareness-filled nothingness, which emptied me of my very self, did the sublime feelings and ineffable truths rush in.

Third, James claims that mystical experiences are short lived, a few minutes, a few hours, nothing more. And not because they're too intense or too taxing on the body but rather the people having these experiences aren't in control of them. They're just not in charge, which brings us to the fourth and final sign: passivity. These mystical folks, they not only encountered deep truths about the universe, they also reported having felt the unmistakable presence of a "superior power" in their midst, a power in whose company they felt involuntarily though not reluctantly held. It was an encounter with an Other so powerful that it tended to "modify the inner life of the subject," wrote James, and for some reason it comforted me to know that. No, it wasn't exactly what I had felt on Pacaya. Mine was more of a communion than an

encounter, though I did call it an "encounter with a God mysterious" on more than one occasion. And I wouldn't have used a
phrase like "superior power" because that would have implied that
I was still me there on that mountain, that Steve was still Steve,
that the superior power was the superior power, all of us distinct,
roped off by our skin like countries on a map. No, it wasn't exactly
the same, but it was close. The folks in James' study, they felt their
experiences had been more than just a knowledge game, that there
was something cosmic and interactive about it all, and once I realized they too had been wrestling with metaphors and imagery to
try to touch the slippery truth of their experience, I felt confident
that if only we could have cut through the fog of language, we
would have seen that we were all standing on common ground.

In James, I found relief. There had been times when I'd tried
to describe Pacaya to others and they'd chimed in with trips of
their own: the joy of relaxing on a beach in Mexico, the wonder
surrounding the pyramids, a dazzling night in Paris. Between their
words lived the suggestion that in Pacaya, I was simply awakening
to the allure of travel, maybe the allure of backpacking in particular. But that never sat well with me because what they didn't know,
and what I didn't know how to tell them without sounding arro-
gant, was that I'd been traveling the world for years. I'd been to the
hotspots they mentioned: Paris, Rome, Athens, Madrid, Florence,
and yes, the pyramids of Giza. I'd also made my way down some of
the roads less travelled: Turkey, Tahiti, Colombia, Morocco, Fiji,
Nicaragua, Rhodes. About 40 countries in all. Come to think of
it, Pacaya wasn't even my first volcano: Years earlier, I'd hiked up
Mount Vesuvius with my then-wife, Sherri, and we'd marvelled at
the volcanic steam pouring out of its cracks as we looked out over
Sorrento and the Tyrrhenian Sea. And as for backpacking, there
was no shortage of stories.

There was that time my friend Sam and I had gone to Panama, had gotten lost in the jungle actually, and taken in by an elderly Hispanic woman who offered us her son's bedroom for the night. The next morning, after a fine breakfast of fried plantains, she instructed her son to escort us to our destination, Mono Feliz, a ramshackle beach lodge routinely visited by endangered squirrel monkeys and built and run by a shaggy American ex-pat who went by the name Juancho. It turns out Juancho became a diehard surfer with an eye for Panama just about the time Americans were learning about a little place on the other side of the globe called Vietnam. It also turns out our escort's name was Oswaldo, who happened to be the sole employee at Juancho's monkey lodge, and to whom Juancho had secretly deeded Mono Feliz upon his death—so we learned from Juancho late one night over beers. We slept in a lean-to overlooking the Pacific. The waves crashing, the sun rising, the fact that there was no electricity, no cell coverage for miles: There on that beach, I knew peace. But it was a worldly peace, a peace that comes from the absence of conflict rather than the presence of Something.

Then there was the time Sam, my brother Mike, and I happened to backpack across Nicaragua the same week the former Sandinista revolutionary Daniel Ortega reclaimed the country's presidency. In Leon, the cultural capital of the country, the director of the municipal theater flagged me down in the street and waved me into his house. Outside flew the flag of the Sandinistas. Wearing only a pair of cut-off jeans, the director took great pride in showing me the collection of theatrical masks that hung on his wall, masks he'd designed and crafted himself and which apparently held a kind of celebrity status in Leon. His English was as bad as my Spanish, but he let it be known: Today was a great day. Daniel Ortega was President once again, this time elected democratically.

The mood was altogether different when we arrived in Laguna de Perlos, a lawless outpost 200 miles East of Leon, where the very elderly and the very young carried spiked clubs to protect themselves against teen gangs. Apparently, the gangs ravaged the town at night in search of the stores of cocaine being staged for cigarette-boat transport to America. "Honesty sticks," they called them, these bats with spikes nailed through them, the instrument of choice for doling out justice in a region of the world bereft of a formal legal system. It was in Laguna de Perlos that we encountered a dozen men carrying heavy supplies and heavier purpose. We asked them what they were up to. "Freedom fighters," they said in broken English. Daniel Ortega was President once again, so they were headed to the mountains of Honduras to join the movement that was planning his overthrow, just as their fathers' generation had done in the 1980s when they were secretly backed by Ollie North and the Reagan administration.

No, I'm no stranger to travel. But none of those trips rose above the realm of adventure, romance, cultural immersion, meaningful times with family and friends. Pacaya was different. It unfolded beyond the grasp of ordinary time. It tore something open in me. That's not an exaggeration. It did something physical to me, damn near traumatized me, left a wake of consequence in my life that no dazzling night in Paris ever had. I left behind my work as a scholar because of Pacaya, and with that, much of my identity. I cancelled a book project on metaphor in modern science, a project to which I'd already devoted a year, so I could read up on creative nonfiction with the hope of learning how to better convey and even think about these spiritual experiences. Pacaya wasn't just more beautiful than Tahiti, wasn't just more adventurous than Nicaragua, more serene than the seaside villages dotting the Italian Mediterranean. It was something else altogether, and James' book gave me the language to begin to describe it: It was noetic, it was ineffable, it left me passive in a freefall into divine love, ultimately it was my first mystical experience, though I still find it hard to use that word, "mystical," in conversations beyond these letters.

In James, I'd found a vocabulary that helped me distinguish Pacaya from all the rest, but it wasn't until Johnston's *Christian Zen* that I found a home. Johnston was an Irish priest sent to Japan in the 1950s to convert the defeated, only to fall in love with their Zen ways. He spoke of a new world afforded by Zen meditation, a world that "offered direct experience of reality without the baggage of analytical thinking and discursive reasoning" and of an "intuitive consciousness that sees things whole, not piecemeal." *Direct experience. Intuitive consciousness. Whole, not piecemeal.* I underlined those phrases, circling "whole," for here was someone giving linguistic soil to the inner life that had broken open in me on Pacaya, a life that continues to spill out onto the shores of Lake Ontario during my wordless trances.

I soon learned that "discursive" was code for reason, logic, the part of us that processes things by breaking them into their constituent parts and studying those parts: their nature, their relationship to each other, their relationship to parts cleaved from other wholes. It's the discursive side of our mind that perceives similarity, difference, order, analogies. It can evaluate arguments, mathematical equations, distances on a map. Years ago, it was the discursive side of me that noticed similarities between the branching of trees in the forest and the branching of bronchioles in the lungs, and wondered whether the same mathematics governed both creations. In fact, for the first thirty-something years of my life, my discursive mind was the only mind I knew.

If the discursive chews reality into manageable bits, the nondiscursive swallows things whole. As Johnston made clear, it encounters things directly, it senses without interpretation, it interacts with the world without first pulling it apart, and as such, its mental impressions are ineffable: Beyond the grasp of thought and language, they are literally inconceivable, and yet they live long and healthy lives in the circuitry of human consciousness, gated off from the discursive world of words and pictures. It was the nondiscursive that, as reported in Matsuo Basho's *A Zen Wave*, led an anonymous eighth-century Japanese poet to write of Mt. Fuji:

> It baffles the tongue.
> It cannot be named.
> It is a god mysterious.

And it was the nondiscursive that animated Aristotle to famously inscribe in his *Metaphysics*:

> For as the eyes of bats
> are to the blaze of day
> so is the reason in our soul
> to the things which are by nature
> most evident of all.

Yes, that's the trouble: The nondiscursive mind creates mental impressions that are inconceivable but never forgotten, like a magical ex-lover you just can't shake. Maybe that's why it's so much easier to say what the nondiscursive mind isn't than what it is, a method known in religious circles as "via negativa": The nondiscursive mind is not thinking, not feeling, not symbolizing at all. It's not the feeling you get in the dentist's chair, gas mask strapped to your nose. It's not a waking dream, not sleep walking, not a coma or death. You can never put your finger on it because it just doesn't track with thinking as we know it, but it does track deeply, powerfully, immediately with the flow of existence. Somewhere between living it and naming it, you'll find the nondiscursive mind, and when you do, be ready for a transformation. That's the common message from my reading so far—from the mystics of James' study to Johnston's meditative life in Japan to my own hike up Pacaya.

My mystical experience atop Pacaya, I think it was this: For the first time in my life, I'd engaged reality using the nondiscursive side of my mind. Having slipped the bonds of thought, I entered into the wholeness of reality, no chewing involved. And when I returned to conscious life and the symbols started flying, my discursive side feverishly tried to make sense of what had just happened and yet it failed to come up with anything but nothing, Nothing, NOTHING! Out of all this mess, one thing is clear. It was the mental registering of the happening and not the happening itself that was mystical. In other words, I think mystical experiences only emerge after the fact. They're what's left to our senses, to our memory, to a bewildered mind after our nondiscursive side has had its way with the universe. While I was in the moment on Pacaya, there was no mystical experience unfolding, there was no experience of any kind, because there was no me, no it, no knowledge of the happening at all. It just happened, it just was. Only after the fact, only when the chewing started, did the labeling and paltry sense-making set in, my discursive mind muddying up the whole adventure as it tried to manufacture an "experience."

I'd lived my whole life enveloped in symbols. I'd grunted to communicate with my parents, I'd pointed at things I wanted, that single outstretched finger probably the first evidence of a symbol-wielding consciousness bubbling up in me. I'd learned what it meant to color "inside" and "outside" the lines, and years later when someone would fall "in" or "out" of love, I wouldn't just squint my eyes, bamboozled by this adult talk. I would get it. I would actually comprehend the meaning of those curious phrases, having learned how to ride the slippery tentacles of a metaphor. I'd also learned how to put people in their boxes: Lisa was good looking, Tom was slow, Gabrielle was a foreigner, and I was Catholic. Whatever else we were, we were these things first, and it painted all of our interactions. I'd gone on to learn the written symbols of the English language, which united the aural with the most powerful sense we have, the visual. This explosion of literacy, it allowed me to follow longer chains of reasoning by inspecting the language there on the page or visualizing it in my mind, seeing its beauty, its gradations, its occasional contradictions. I was able to picture knowledge and remember and manipulate those pictures, which turned out to be an important passport into mathematics and geography and physics and philosophy, into Bach and Mach and Feynman and Newton and Auden and Aristotle and Jesus. And with one wave of the hand, Pacaya took it all away. It was as if that fiery volcano had stuffed all my symbols into a grenade and pulled the pin: In that moment, I was no longer human, no longer *homo symbolicus* as they say, and the world soon pulsed with a new kind of meaning.

Johnston knew all about the grenade throwing. In his book, he wrote that Zen meditation, which looks an awful lot like the wordless chanting I've been doing down by the lake (minus the pillow and leg pretzeling), anyhow, that Zen meditation was a kind of silent sitting that rested on "detachment from the very process of thinking, from the images and ideas and conceptualization that are so dear to Western man. And through this detachment one is introduced to a deep and beautiful realm of psychic life," a realm he would later call the *silentium mysticum*. Johnston had long admired the statues he found lining the sacred spaces in Japan, statues of enlightened Buddhas and Bodhisattvas "rapt in deep silence, in nothingness, in unknowing." In those beautiful pieces of art, he saw an Eastern parallel to the lost contemplative tradition that had once animated his own religion: a parallel to the forgotten theology of medieval mystics like St. John of the Cross, the 16th century Spanish priest who found the "blind stirring of love" in the depths of his own wordless sitting, and to the anonymous author of *The Cloud of Unknowing*, a 14th century English prayer book for Christians craving pure union with their Creator.

Over the centuries, thought Johnston, Christians had come to place so much emphasis on the discursive side of religious consciousness—on studying the scriptures and memorizing the prayers—that they'd lost touch with the *silentium mysticum*, the "deep interior silence" that had once graced the contemplative lives of their ancestors, Christians who believed God was beyond all symbols. These moments of interior silence, they weren't just private vacations to a land of bliss: It was in their depths that such prized virtues as faith, empathy, and character were born and sustained. He wrote of the many great Zen practitioners he knew, all of whom insisted that there is no other, no self, that beneath symbol and desire and the will to survive there is only Oneness. He wrote of one Buddhist friend in particular: When asked by Johnston to describe his theology, the friend replied, "Do you really think that you can talk about nothingness, emptiness, or the void? Do you really think you can talk about God? Of course you can't. You are part of the void; you are part of nothingness; you are part of God. All is one." If Zen could drop these Buddhists into their nondiscursive mind, it could do the same for Christians. Johnston was sure of it. So sure, he spent the rest of his life teaching Zen as a way of reviving the Christian heart, for it was in the nothingness of deep contemplation that the Holy Spirit could once again roam free.

I kept reading. What Johnston found in sitting, Belden Lane found in the austere landscapes of the wild. So compelling was his writing, so deft his decoding of the parabled history between land

and spirit, that by the time I was ten pages into his *Solace of Fierce Landscapes* I got the distinct feeling that anyone who could fog a mirror would have known, predicted even, that my first mystical experience would take place on a mountain. And if not a mountain, then a desert. Pacaya, I reckoned, was both: Jutting 8,300 feet into the sky, it was a mountain, yes, but not a lush one. Above the tree line, its conifers gave way to a sun-punished moonscape as barren as any desert, precisely the kind of unforgiving terrain that for millennia has been inspiring out-of-body experiences among trekkers of all religions. "Out on the edge—in the desert waste or suspended between earth and sky," wrote Lane, we "transgress the limits of culture, language, all the personal boundaries by which [our] lives are framed. In whatever form one may find it, 'the desert loves to strip us bare,' as Saint Jerome insisted." It is only then, when we are stripped bare, wrote Lane, when "we abandon every effort to control God by experiencing God, relinquishing even the grasping self (always anxious to add the Deity to its store of personal acquisitions), that the mystery of meeting God beyond experience ever becomes possible."

This connection between mountains and mysticism, I'd somehow managed to miss it all these years. I'd missed the fact that the Carmelites, a religious order within the Roman Catholic Church, could trace its origin all the way back to the desert hermits living on Mount Carmel in the 12th century, themselves self-proclaimed citizens of an uninterrupted line of monks who had lived on the mountain since Elijah, the famed prophet who made Mount Carmel his base for contemplation 2,000 years earlier. They were not sitting lotus style like Johnston and his Japanese friends, but they were entering into what sounded like the same nondiscursive space by way of their interaction with the barren land. I'd missed the fact that it was on a mountain that Moses received the Ten Commandments, that Jesus was transfigured, that the Qur'an was revealed to Muhammad. I'd missed the centrality of Mt. Kailash, Mt. Athos, and Mt. Koya-san to many of the world's religions. The list went on: From Anthony of Egypt to Charles de Foucauld to St. John of the Cross to Evagrius, Lane chronicled the powerful interplay of desolate landscapes and religious experience, offering a kind of literary fugue on Ortega y Gasset's theme, "Tell me the landscape in which you live, and I will tell you who you are." The details didn't matter, not the who lived where and when and under the banner of which religion. What I found absolutely astonishing was this: Our relationship with God can be predictably shaped—somewhat *controlled* even—by such an arbitrary thing as the terrain on which we stand.

I need to get back to mountains. They feel like the most sacred thing on earth, these portals into pure union with the divine. I need to reflect on these ideas in their company, bring the knowledge I gained from these two months of reading to bear against the experience of being there, witnessing. Last week, I ceremoniously returned Lane's book to my shelf, and booked a flight to India. I'll be wandering the Himalayas by Christmas.

CROSSED INTO NEPAL ON FOOT with nowhere to stay and no map to speak of, in search of the *silentium mysticum* I'd found on Pacaya. If such an experience could be had in the war-torn highlands of Guatemala, I reasoned, how much more would be possible among the saffron sunsets and majestic peaks of the Himalayas?

It was a logic I would come to regret.

I crossed at Belahiya, a frantic border town full of armed soldiers and dust. Dust that lounged in the air, harassing every nose and mouth that walked by. And the soldiers? They donned black surgical masks, each and every one of them, as they stood alongside the road, purpose unknown. All nice people I'm sure, despite the eerie fusion of anonymity and rifles, but the other side of silence this was not.

I made my way to Tansen, a mountainside village of Newari heritage, where I awoke one morning to a silence so still all I could hear was a faint ringing in my ears (probably from Belahiya). No car horns, no bird chirps, not even a wind-heckled window to disrupt me. It was time, I thought. Time to step into and through the silence that stretched before me. I had traveled 7,000 miles for this. I was ready.

I laid in bed and made not a move, but far from emptying me of my discursive self, the silence gave breath to my thoughts. They coursed along the inner landscape of my mind, slot racing at first in rigorous, analytic lines, then gliding like skaters on fresh morning ice. Kepler's laws of planetary motion, ferns of frost growing on a midnight window, Simon and Garfunkel, the nature of dust: This is what I thought of. You know, the things that flow down the stream of consciousness in moments of uncommon lucidity, taking you from John Paul II to John Paul Jones to the John and Paul you grew up with all in a heartbeat or two, before pinballing you to another quadrant of your life. I listened to my breathing, and imagined the day it would stop. Would it be a surprise? Would I see it coming? I thought of the beauty locked in the dark woods of the walls that surrounded me, I thought of the many forms of beauty I had seen in the world, and then I thought of thought itself, and thoughts of thoughts of thought. I thought of hardship and heartbreak, I thought of my childhood and embarrassment, I thought of many things, but I never thought of love. Yes, they brought insight, these gymnastic thoughts, but here I was trying to enter the place hidden from thought, where the many streams of existence flow true and unabated, and what does my mind do? It gives itself leave to roam, to expand, eventually to walk around like a peacock inspecting and picking at the carnage of my life locked away at memory's edge. What I would have given for that peacock to grow weary and rest, even to sleep, to allow the *silentium mysticum* to awaken in me if only for a moment. What I would have given to spill out into the universe once again, and enter into the wholeness of reality beyond self. Yes, what I wanted there in Tansen was transcendence; what I got was a quiet hotel room and extra time to think.

I moved on to Pokhara. I'm sure there are towns in Nepal where the peace, the tranquility, the *om-mani-padme-hum* for which the country is known is all but wafting through the streets. Pokhara is not one of them. I entered the town on foot so I wouldn't miss a thing, and found nothing more than wifi cafes and pizza parlors and barber shops and laundromats and hotels and pubs and banks. Some traded on the Buddha's likeness, all advertised in English. Signs screamed "Authentic Newari food", "Authentic Tibetan rugs," "Hamburgers." Kids handed out coupons on the street. At least in Tansen, "namaste," the universal Nepali greeting, meant just that. In Pokhara, it meant "buy a rug" or "look at this hand-made flute."

I decided I needed altitude. Rarefied air. An unobstructed view of the Himalayas. So I searched my guidebook for the highest place around—it turned out to be Mount Sarangkot—and took a cab up to its base. From there, I began the hike up. I didn't have a destination in mind, just higher and higher. I kept thinking of what Belden Lane had written: That it is out on the edge—in the midst of a desert or high atop a mountain—where we escape our culture, our language, our self. By late afternoon, I had made it to a modest mustard farm overlooking the Western Himalayas, where a middle-aged Nepali man offered me lodging in a small cinderblock cabin next to his goats. His name was Balrum, and as I would soon learn, he had been sent home to die.

*   *   *

We Americans have our restaurants and TVs. The men and women of Nepal, their campfires. Campfires alongside the road, campfires in the backyard. Campfires before working the mustard fields, campfires long after. These are not the large, log campfires of North America. A bit of kindling and brush will do. It is the campfire that cements daily life for the people on Mount Sarangkot. It is their site for solidarity.

My first night on Sarangkot, I was invited to such a fire. After settling into my cabin, I had returned to the main house in search of food and maybe some company, and I had found Balrum, the owner of the farm, a man of maybe 45, sitting on the porch playing solitaire. He introduced me to his wife, who didn't speak English, and explained that she was in charge of food for the family and guests. Then we sat and talked of mountain life, and of Nepal, while I ate. His English was excellent, even his choice of idioms, and the food was home grown: Lentils and spices and greens and tomatoes taken right from their garden and combined in simple ways to create hearty soups, salads, and goulash-type dishes, all vegetarian. After some time Balrum stood and gestured for me to follow as he made his way to a clearing where he arranged a few plastic chairs around a small pit and lit a fire. Others soon joined us, and we sat and drank tea and talked quietly as the white peaks of the Himalayas raged into the dusk. To my left was Balrum's daughter, Santi, seventeen years old and home from college. To my right, Balrum's wife and a skittish Austrian backpacker named George who was also renting a cabin on the property. Across from me was Balrum, witling a piece of wood, tending to the fire.

The conditions were perfect: the mood, the mountains, the peace and quiet, the people. I was sure the next morning, I would slip into the Great Nothingness and say goodbye to my discursive mind for as long as the mountains would have it. But first, I thought, a bit of socializing.

I leaned over to Santi and asked why she was not at college.

"My father is dying," she said. "He has called me home."

It's been three months since that night, and I can still see Santi sitting there. Her erect posture. Her nervous hands. You could just see the hope and the fear battling for priority in the sheen of her eyes.

"It's his blood." She had a dramatic way of saying it. Bluuuud. "His bluud is bad. In his neck. I tried to give him my bluud but they wouldn't take it. Said it would just run out of him, on the inside. His bluud is leaking out, and it's poisoning him."

Something pierced me. I held my eyes on Santi's as she leaned in closer and continued.

"My brother's in England, and we can't afford to bring him home, so he calls everyday, everyday asking about my father. The clinic gave my mother some pills for his pain, and said that he will soon grow weak. Then he won't be able to walk. That's when she should start the pills. And then it will be difficult for him to breath, and then he'll pass out, and he won't wake up. It's his bluud. I tried to give him my bluud, you know, I tried, but they wouldn't take it. They said it would just leak out."

She looked at me as if I could do something, her eyes weathered by life into polished stones.

"Santi, do you have people you can talk to—friends, family, I don't know—to help you through this?" It was the only thing I could think to ask that wouldn't make things worse.

"Not my friends. But my mother. And my father." She nodded.

I nodded too, relieved she wouldn't be enduring this alone, and then I looked over at Balrum. He was sitting back enjoying the fire, and alight all right, but by the fire of his own contentment. A slight smile spread across his face, and he nodded gently as if to say, "Welcome to this part of my life."

We spent the rest of the night talking in twos, Balrum and George, Santi and me. Santi talked of college, and of life on the mountain, and the fact that this was her father's mountain in a way, that he'd lived here his whole life and had left only twice— once for a government meeting in Kathmandu, and once for the clinic—and how she worried now about her future and her mother's future and the future of the farm. I'm usually a talker, but that night I listened.

*   *   *

The next morning, I was too shaken to seek out the *silentium mysticum*. The news of Balrum's impending death cast a morose hue over the whole of the Himalayas, and the morning sun, which usually spilled ochre and saffron and hope and adventure onto an awaiting sky, now only reminded me of his blood. His bluud. He would be gone soon. Under the slow arc of a sanguine sun, he would wheeze and gasp and then he would be silent. He would be—the word brings anxiety to me even now—he would be exsanguinated, drained of blood by the beating of his own heart until his heart could bear it no more.

I made my way to the only society within reach, Balrum's porch. There I met Yuri, a middle aged man from Russia who had been meditating in one of Balrum's ridgeline cabins for 45 days. He had come out for tea. Next to him were Balrum and Santi playing cards, and George.

"So where are you traveling?" George asked, starting up the usual traveler's talk. I hadn't learned much about George, and I got the sense that was just how George liked it, so I offered him little in return.

"Landed in India and made my way here," I explained as I steeped my tea. "I plan on heading on to Kathmandu, and then back to India to catch my flight home in two weeks."

"Not possible." His words fell like bricks, sharp and definite.

"What do you mean?" I asked.

"Once you leave India, you cannot return for two months." George sipped his tea, seemingly bored.

"What, what do you mean?" I asked again, abrupt this time as if to shake loose a different set of words from his mouth.

"They have a rule, the Indian government. You can't just come and go. Once you leave, you have to wait two months, and then you can return."

My head lowered under the weight of his words, and I peered at him over my glasses. Stuck in Nepal. Stuck in Nepal for two months! The idea folded around my mind, sealing it off from the rest of me.

Then Yuri chimed in. "Don't worry," he said, stirring his tea with a biscuit. "You can stay in my cabin. There's enough space for the two of us."

I turned to Balrum for help, but he was smiling at Yuri's generous offer, smiling at me as if to say, "Welcome to this part of your life." Everyone returned to their tea and cards, the matter seemingly settled, as my body tensed and squeezed around me.

I excused myself and returned to my cabin. I paced inside, then out. I would be stuck in Nepal for two months. I would miss the first half of spring semester. I would miss my loved ones. I would miss my life! Then Balrum's execution played like a movie before me, and I felt guilty even worrying about my own petty problems. My eyes absently took in the mountains, the fields, the baby goats playing nearby as I flipped my circumstances forward and back in my mind, stewing, perseverating, comparing them to Balrum's and telling myself they were nothing compared to his. Yet still I was thistled with anxiety.

As the sun rose higher into the sky, the full weight of my panic suffocated my body, a slow, sweaty constriction that grew from inside my belly. Balrum's death would be an execution, but who

was the executioner? Would I be here for it? I would need money
wired to me to weather the next two months. Would I have a job
when I got home? Would Santi have to drop out of college after
his death? Could I sneak across the Indian border? What was
the penalty for sneaking across the Indian border? Jail? Maybe I
could bribe someone. What was the penalty for bribing someone
to sneak across the Indian border? Worse than the penalty for
sneaking across the Indian border? Could I fly to China? My
mind churned away at the uncertainties, the angles, the twists and
contortions that might make it all right, and I was afraid it would
not know how to stop. I tried to meditate, but was assailed by
grotesque images of death, not only Balrum's but the fabricated
deaths of loved ones back home. I would miss their funerals, my
mind quickly pronounced, and I had to remind myself that no
one back home was dying. Just Balrum. And then I'd feel guilty for
even thinking that way, for steadying myself in the knowledge that
it was Balrum's life that was disintegrating and not mine—and yet
Balrum seemed happier than I was. He was playing cards with his
daughter, he was having warm conversations with his wife, he was
enjoying sunsets around the fire, smiling, all the while smiling.
Soon a new fear appeared and mixed with the others: that my
mind had buckled, was wrecked forever. Maybe it had all been
too much for me atop this mountain, stuck in this country. We
all have limits, I told myself, and rarely did I respect mine. If man
is a thinking reed as Pascal once said, then maybe mine had just
been snapped. Maybe it had all finally caught up with me. Justice.

Time passed mysteriously that morning. An hour would
speed by in minutes, then three minutes would stretch like taffy
as I faced the isolation and anxiety that spilled forth from a place
unknown. Over and over, I tried to pick the lock to my own sanity
but failed. And in my failing, life squeezed even harder.

Somewhere in all of this, Yuri came into view and invited me to his cabin for incense and a fire. The cabin wasn't much to look at. An 8 by 10 foot room with a small bed and a table that steadied a few candles and sticks of incense. With uncommon precision, he lit one stick and placed it in its holder, then stood back and admired the fingers of sweet smoke that rose to meet us. As we sat on the floor, he gestured for me to breathe deeply. I felt like praying for Balrum but scuttled the thought, knowing I needed space from his gravity.

Yuri was about as languid as the smoke we were inhaling, and both calmed me. His eyes shone the way Santi's should have, and he had the levity of a child. I told him about Pacaya, about my slipping beneath language and finding a kind of communion. He smiled, and gave me a knowing nod. Of course he did. He had been meditating in a Himalayan mountain shack for a month and a half. He must have known a thing or two about the *silentium mysticum*. As soon as I realized that, there was no need to talk. We simply allowed time to unfold before us.

After a while, he walked over to his door and lit a fire just beyond it, in the dirt where a welcome mat would be. "There is no I and you, there is only we," he said in all seriousness before turning a watery gaze to the Himalayas. "See that man plowing the mustard field? We are plowing the mustard field," he said. Yuri was a man of wide intelligence, a professional back in Moscow, but one of no particular standing, I soon surmised, since he was accustomed to saying things like "A man who wants is a man at war with himself" and "Are we not all One, the humans, the birds, the sky unending?" And of course there was the small impracticality of his silent sitting for months on end, his just being. This is not the kind of guy you put in charge of your firm's new accounts.

He showed me his collection of teas, his singing bowl, his incense—all designed to facilitate his journey to the other side.

He thumbed his radio, the kind with a hanger for an antenna, and tuned it to Nepali public radio. A sweet concoction of bells and drums and female vocals soon mixed with the incense and the heat of the rising day and the melancholy there on the mountain, and we sat on the ground and stared into the flame for a long time. I thought of Balrum again, this time reaching beyond the fear to prayer. I thought of Yuri too, a man I had immediately admired— only now my emotions flared because in him I was starting to see myself in ten years' time if I chose to continue on my present path: alone, in self-imposed exile, in search of my next transcendental fix. I had chosen to leave my family for Christmas, after all. How much of a stretch was it to think of leaving for a season, a year, in search of that something less than nothing? For years, the idea of a Yuri had thrilled me. Since Pacaya, it had seemed the culmination of the kind of spiritual life I wanted to lead. But as I sat next to him and took in the reality of such an existence, it struck me, for an instant, as incomplete. A day, a weekend, yes, but a month, a season, a year? Slowly, my admiration mixed with a kind of sadness as I imagined the life and loved ones he had left behind in Moscow. He was a charismatic man, a man of obvious intelligence, with an intense yet warm personality: He had so much to offer the world. Surely they missed him back home. Surely Moscow was the worse for his silent sitting for months on end in one of Balrum's little cabins.

Balrum. He had a different way of moving through the world, one that brought him closer to the living. That smile of his, it wasn't a symptom of resignation, nor was he in denial of the death that awaited him. No, it was the smile of a man in total acceptance of the reality that flowed before him and through him and all around him. And it allowed him, in the midst of his whole world collapsing, to be present and wholly engaged in a card game with his daughter, in a quiet conversation with his wife, in the solitude that comes with living on the mountain. Whereas Yuri and I wanted to orbit the earth, Balrum seemed content to plant himself on it and live in full relationship with those around him. His was an everyday spirituality, not nearly as epic as Yuri's, but in the end, more memorable. He seemed capable of enjoying the fullness of reality, and he didn't have to leave his thoughts, his country, or himself to do it.

There was a goodness to Balrum that I will never be able to describe other than to say he was brilliant the way a wheat field is in the setting sun. If I had to guess, I'd say there were times when he had not a single expectation coursing through those veins of his, and in those times he was able to rhythm in tune with daily life whereas Yuri and I seemed to be jockeying for position against it.

Somewhere in the night, long after I thanked Yuri for his hospitality and returned to my cabin, I felt them. All the expectations I had: that I would live a long and healthy life, that those I loved would love me in return, that I would outlive my parents and my children would outlive me, that life owed me something, by God, it owed me a sound mind and clean teeth and my next breath and a job that would stay steady and not disintegrate with the economy, and passage back to India and a healthy sex life, please God, a healthy sex life, and ultimately, the expectation that if I could just cajole the world into helping me meet all these expectations, to meet them for one short moment, that happiness would descend on me like a dove and stay with me and over time become mine. I could see these expectations, and I could see Balrum had none of them. What was then only a mist of awareness, an intuition, I can now articulate as this: It wasn't the trip that was going wrong, it was my expectation, and in the gulf between them lay my misery. I sat with that mist for a long time that night, and then went to bed.

The next morning, I imagined them brittle and falling away, my expectations. They fell like the icicles of my youth, me on the porch with the broom. It might have been a mental exercise at first, but then I felt it in my body. My center of being had shifted from my head to my abdomen. My shoulders were now above me. I don't know what else to say other than I felt my biology, I was no longer locked inside my head, and I experienced something new. It wasn't exactly stepping through to the other side of silence, but it was this: With the help of the mountains that morning and the urgency I felt in my circumstances and the image of Balrum ever smiling before me, his impending death nonetheless out there on the horizon, I came to feel no expectation, not one, and a stillness washed over me. The first thing I did, I marvelled at my own breathing. The experience of each inhale, one, two, three, each one a drop of life. Then I thought of Balrum, and what came to mind was that he was a lucky man: Up there in his house spending time with his family on this beautiful morning, probably drinking tea and talking with Santi and smiling. A sense of contradiction jostled me: How could I say he was lucky when he was about to die? But as I tried again to melt all expectation, again I felt it: Balrum was lucky, I was lucky, we were all lucky that morning. We were breathing, we were alive, we were part of the Mystery.

'VE DECIDED TO STOP RELYING ON BOOKS to help me make sense of my mountaintop experiences. I need to understand them in my own terms, in whose reflection I'll feel a sense of belonging, authenticity, since I know full well I'll be living with them for the rest of my life.

I keep thinking of a lecture I once attended by the great Japanese writer Kenzaburo Oe. When asked why we should read, he said, "To make the words of our ancestors our own." A fine answer, but one that seems far too dangerous to me now. Why should I ask my ancestors what Pacaya and Balrum and Yuri mean? How can I be sure I wouldn't simply parrot their answers when thinking through the details of my life? And how is that not a recipe for disaster, a roadmap to living among the walking dead, knowingly estranging myself from my own life through the sloppy ingestion of language not mine?

Even now, I wonder about that last line in my previous letter: "We were breathing, we were alive, we were part of the Mystery." I heard something very similar to that at Plum Village, France, when Thich Nhat Hanh gave a lecture on interbeing. Did my experience in Nepal that morning really summon those words in me? Or did Thich Nhat Hanh's words simply come to mind, and I chose them because they were preformed, convenient, and close enough? I can never be sure.

In college, I read parts of St. Augustine's Confessions, and one part still terrifies me: the part where he laments having focused so intensely on the great works of literature that he failed to recognize the longings of his own heart. I admire Oe, but I'm not about to make Augustine's mistake. I know I need to reach for language to come to some crust of understanding of what happened on Pacaya, what happened in Nepal when all my expectations fell away, what happens even now as I meditate down by the lake. I know I need to reach for language to understand what changed in me when I sat with Yuri by the fire and questioned whether his life was really complete. But I'm not about to fashion a spirituality out of the linguistic fabric of others. Instead, I'm going inward— no books, no TV, no radio—to see what I can find.

CAN FEEL MYSELF UNDERGOING a fundamental change in how I relate to my mind and body.

I'd always thought of myself as living a few inches behind my eyes, just above my ears. That's where the meaning happened, so that's where I lived my life. The body was but a shell, and I used to go weeks without thinking about it. Don't get me wrong: I worked out, I brushed my teeth, I polished my shell in all the culturally appropriate ways, but as far as developing a conscious relationship with it or feeling that it was an important part of who I was, that just didn't happen.

About the only time I paid attention to my body was when it was failing me and therefore taxing my mind. Like the time I drown in high school, and a friend of a friend pulled me from the lake's midnight blackness, dragged me to shore, and resuscitated me there on the beach. For the next two days, I had a hard time understanding where my limbs and head were relative to the rest of me. I felt as if my head might bump into a china plate or a closed door six feet away if only I nodded in that direction. And not because it would stretch that far or detach and roll down the hall. No, the perception owed to a less logical, other worldly awareness that didn't acknowledge space and size as we know them. It was not pretty. I imagine cases of oxygen deprivation seldom are. And you can bet that for about 48 hours my body was thrust front and center into the jaws of a frantic mind.

Then there was the time a sloppy pickup truck driver ran a stop sign—actually accelerated through the stop sign according to one witness—and crashed into my car, fating my head to shatter the windshield. The cop who arrived on the scene took one look at the wreckage that used to be my Sentra and asked, "Is this your car?" I nodded from the sidewalk, staring at it in mild disbelief. "Son, you just won the lottery. You should be dead," he informed me. I nodded again and in a way that showed him I understood the gravity of the situation, then declined medical care and walked home with just a bit of blood trickling down my hairline. But the next morning—and that morning alone, thank God—my speech was delayed. I knew what I wanted to say, but the words just took their time coming out, sometimes a whole second or two late. That might not sound like much, but when you want to talk, two seconds is more than enough time to get you thinking about your corporeal existence.

And while these traumas got me in touch with my body, they did little to cleave my self from my mind: When I lost track of my body in space, when I frantically awaited my delinquent speech to pass my lips, the I was still the same I as before: The self that shacked up with the mind in seemingly natural cohabitation just behind my eyes. Only now my mind-self was judge, my body the hapless defendant.

That's all changing now. The more I meditate down by the lake, the more I feel my center of being—is that my self?—drop into my abdomen, just like it did when I was in Nepal. (Did I just refer to myself in the third person, as "it"? Strange, trying to weld language to these experiences.) When I'm down in my abdomen, my head feels like an appendage of sorts, an important one of course what with all its symbol making capabilities and what-not, but an appendage of me rather than me per se.

As I make the journey to my abdomen, I sometimes feel my shoulders rise up behind me and my sense of self expand to roughly the size of a half-inflated soccer ball. A somewhat flattened soccer ball resting just above my beltline. Often times, that's when I drop into a mystical experience. It's rarely as powerful and dramatic as that first time on Pacaya, but it's in the same vicinity. The world I find, it's sublime, it's as exciting as it is peaceful, but then I make the mistake of thinking about it, realizing it's happening. The symbols start flying, and that thrusts me back into my head, my mind and self reunited once again, and the mystery vanishes.

What do you make of this, this thing I've come to call "body traveling"?

CAN'T GET PROCRUSTES OUT OF MY HEAD, that strange character from Greek mythology who would invite passersby to his home for the evening, and once there, strap them to his bed. If their legs were too long, he would chop them off; if they were too short, he would stretch them. It's such a diabolical tale, and for the longest time, I couldn't figure out why I kept thinking of it, this myth I hadn't thought of in 15 years.

Then it hit me: Procrustes is the discursive mind personified. In order to make sense of the complexities of life, in order to make "experiences" at all, we build an elaborate infrastructure of concepts—"dog," "God," "road," "democracy," "evil"—whose meanings remain stable over time and place, and it's in the reflection of those concepts that we enter into discursive consciousness. I'd never linked Procrustes to this, but once it hit me, yes, there's a lot of chopping and stretching going on as we contort our lives to fit our ideas, as we pour our visceral present into our conceptual past.

I used to try to think about my church without thinking of it as a church, you know? I'd try to really remember what I'd experienced last Sunday: the bricks and mortar and cracks in the foundation and smell of dust and must and the well-placed telephone wire stapled discreetly along the floor, my heart rate and breathing and the feel of my clothes against my skin, the feeling of air, the feeling of my blinking, the tension in my neck. I could do it for a few seconds, but then my mind would get rattled and reach for an orienting concept—"church"—and suddenly the inchoate experience was lost.

Mark Twain wrote about this Procrustean malfeasance in his classic *Life on the Mississippi*. All the grace and beauty of the river was lost, he said, once he became a riverboat pilot and "mastered the language of this water." The sun, the moon, the eddies and ripples: What had once brought him to rapture were now merely signs for navigation, his expertise as a pilot forever stripping him of his mystical relationship with the earth.

There are nights when I understand the necessity of concepts, the miracle of words: The fact that we can model our reality through concepts, and in their reflection, enter into consciousness. And then writing, this technology that allows us to graphically depict those concepts, to work with them and modify them there on the page, to move them around and create new concepts that would never have been discoverable through speech alone.

But there are nights when I think of Procrustes and Twain and my church experiment and living in the wake of Pacaya and think: Concepts, they are diabolical. They trap me in the prisonhouse of language and divorce me from the Great Unnameable that I know to be pulsating in the moments between time, calling to me, calling to all of us to join in the same mystical oneness that lit the stars. Concepts separate us from God, plain and simple.

MY RETURN TO GUATEMALA LAST MONTH was, of course, glorious. It was with my friend Sam and a handful of students from the university where I teach. We explored remote Mayan villages and slept in uncomfortable hostels and met curious people from around the world in buses, boats, and questionable gringo dives. We learned about the Guatemalan war and history from community leaders dedicated to alleviating rural poverty. And we hiked Pacaya.

It's a curious thing to bring a group of people to a place that's so personal and powerful for you. I didn't know what it would mean to them. But when they passed the tree line and entered Pacaya's moonscape, the drudgery of the first half of the hike transformed into glee, energy. Soon they were striking yoga poses on the moonscape, marveling at the jagged horizon. Some held their arms out and looked straight up to the sky, others sat alone on rock outcrops and took in the sum total of their lives. (None of them knew about my own Pacaya experience.)

I took some time to myself, awash in gratitude that life would allow me to bring the next generation of seekers to this place. It was a pilgrimage for me, a transformative experience for all, a routine Spring Break vacation for none. (I've posted the itinerary below in case you want to do it.)

But now, I'm back in Western New York, and the dread of flatland is setting in. Separated from moonscaped mountains, I find myself clinging to my lakeside meditation. I even try to visualize mountains in these meditations. It helps. There is temporary relief, but it's not enough. It's just not enough. I'm tired of the signs, I need the thing signified.

Itinerary for the Great Guatemalan Adventure

Here's the plan, and while it's been methodically organized, we might find ourselves making small changes as the trip unfolds. This is Central America after all. Local festivals (which we'll try to attend) and organized protests (which we won't), along with the weather, are just a few of the factors that might cause us to change it up a bit, all in an attempt to offer you a meaningful, safe adventure.

Sunday: We'll catch the sunrise flight from Buffalo to Guatemala City by way of Atlanta, then hop a bus to the Spanish colonial city of Antigua, where we'll stay for three nights at a backpacker favorite, El Hostal. Dormitory sleeping arrangements; breakfast and wifi included.

Monday: A local guide will take us on a morning walk of Antigua, including stops at City Hall Palace, the Palace of the Captain's General, and the Cathedral and its ruins. The tour will focus on the city's history, culture, and restoration efforts. In the afternoon, you'll be free to explore the city in smaller groups, visit the churches and shops, exchange money, and just stretch your travel legs. We'll all meet back at the hostel for a communal dinner, so a stop at one of Antigua's many markets is essential.

Tuesday: By way of private shuttle, we'll spend the morning visiting nearby villages, including the museum at the Convent/Archbishop's Palace in San Juan del Obispo, daily life in San Pedro las Huertas, and the Maya town of San Antonio Aguas Calientes, known for its authentic Maya textiles. In the afternoon, we'll hike the lush forest and mystical moonscape of Pacaya, an active volcano that rises to an elevation of 8,373 feet. If we're lucky, we'll have a chance to roast marshmallows over rocks heated by underground lava, and experience incredible "above the clouds" views of the surrounding highlands. Be advised: Pacaya is a 2.5 hour (roundtrip), Class II hike; at times, the steep ascent will require you to use your hands to steady yourself.

Wednesday: We'll make the three hour journey from Antigua to Lake Atitlan by private shuttle, hop a boat to Tzununa, a remote Maya village on the northern shore, and settle into the beautiful Lomas de Tzununa by noon. You'll have the afternoon and evening to yourself. Triple occupancy sleeping arrangements; Internet available.

Thursday: After a briefing on Tzununa, one of the poorest communities on Lake Atitlan, we'll be led on a walking tour of the village by one of its primary benefactors, Thierry Delrue, a retired UNICEF officer who was part of the team responsible for implementing the UN Peace Accord in Guatemala after the civil war. Thierry and his wife, Maria Castells-Arrosa, continue to support primary education for the children of Tzununa through fundraising, construction, and liaison work with other organizations. In the afternoon, we'll hop a boat with Thierry to the other side of the lake and hike through the Maya villages of San Juan and San Pablo and the ever-gringo San Pedro la Laguna.

Friday: Led by Thierry or Maria, we'll spend the morning hiking to the remote Maya village of Santa Cruz la Laguna, enjoying panoramic views of Lake Atitlan along the way. We'll stop for lunch and some down time in Santa Cruz before making the hike back. Be advised: This is a 4 hour (roundtrip), Class II hike that includes sections of mountainous terrain with steep vertical drops. This hike requires concentration, and at times you will need to use your hands to steady yourself.

Saturday: We'll make the three hour journey from Lake Atitlan back to Antigua by private shuttle, and settle in at Earth Lodge, a mountain ecolodge that doubles as a avocado farm. In the afternoon, we'll hike to the nearby Guatemalan village of El Hato, and learn about the various educational initiatives underway to improve the lives of El Hato's children. Dormitory and triple occupancy sleeping arrangements; Internet available.

Sunday: We'll say goodbye to Earth Lodge in the early morning, and catch a shuttle to the airport in Guatemala City for our flight back to the States, hopefully with the smell of campfire still on our clothes.

EXPLAIN IT TO MY FRIENDS THIS WAY: Imagine a guy who loved churches, I mean really loved them, for it was in a church that he first felt the intense presence of the holy. So inspired was this guy that he spent all of his spare time in them, especially when they were empty. He would sit in silence, and find himself slipping into contact with Something beneath the occasional creak from the pew, beneath the smell of the incense two days old. It might only last a second or two, but it was pure ecstasy, the discovery of a lifetime this cosmic space between thoughts where, as he would later put it, he encountered a little death that freed him to Life.

When no one was around, this guy would walk the church aisles secure in his wordless existence, gliding his hand along the tops of pews, sometimes taking time to smell with deep satisfaction the plaster walls or the radiators hissing their heat into the void. He loved the howl of the wind against the windows, even the occasional car horn outside. They reminded him of the sanctuary he found inside the church, inside any old-fashioned church actually. But over time, he turned this sanctuary into a prison.

The problem was, the more time he spent in these churches, the less happiness he could find outside of them. At work, at the gym, even in his home life, he grew cold in the long shadow of the fact that he was not at church, not in the arms of what he came to understand as a certain kind of love. When he wasn't at church, he grew cynical and irritable, qualities entirely counter to his nature, and began to take it out on gas station attendants and grocery store cashiers and bank tellers and friends. When he wasn't at church, he obsessed over plans to return to one. He often wondered where the best churches were, the ones that would offer him an even more intense experience. If his favorite on 4th Street, an old gothic cathedral from the turn of the century, would induce such spiritual bliss, what would Notre Dame or St. Peter's do?

He started up a side hobby as a chauffeur, going out of his way to drive all sorts of people to churches, people who couldn't otherwise get there, in the hopes that they too would feel the intense holy he encountered. Driving them home, he would never say too much, only that the church was beautiful or that it was certainly safe and warm inside. But in his heart, the safety and warmth took on cosmic proportions. He even thought about becoming a church caretaker, so he could spend all of his time there. When he wasn't at church, he wasn't himself, and God was simply not there.

That guy is me, only my church is the mountains. And living in flat Western New York, I can see that I'm slowly meeting my demise.

T'S GETTING WORSE. A few years ago, I dreamt of an enormous warehouse made of barn board and metal strapping and long Byzantine windows. It was dimly lit and totally empty save a furious band of sunlight that shone on an elaborate, old-fashioned machine, something that resembled a Victorian era printing press though heavier and haunting, made of cast iron and heavy wood and large, toothy gears a foot in diameter that churned methodically behind puffs of extruding steam. The entire device—this was no contraption—sat center stage in the warehouse, and was under considerable pressure, what with the steam power and all, but it was a pressure that brought it to life rather than crushing it under the weight of work, much the way the ocean's depths bring to life whole ecologies of deep sea creatures that would seize and cease if brought into the timid atmosphere of shallow waters.

The machine shook and wheezed and manufactured a sprocket before my eyes, which slid down a chute and dropped into an awaiting tray with the sound of satisfaction. The machine's mechanical arm slowly swiveled and claimed the sprocket, and installed it on its right side where an old, apparently failing sprocket had functioned for the past many years. It was then that I realized the sole and unwavering purpose of the machine, so finely tuned and efficient: It existed merely to preserve itself.

It was a machine designed to manufacture all the parts it would ever need and nothing more, so it could keep on existing, which allowed it to make more parts, which allowed it to keep on existing, which allowed it to make more parts, which allowed it to keep on existing,

which allowed it to make more parts,
which allowed it to keep on existing,
which allowed it to make more parts,
which allowed it to keep on existing,
which allowed it to make more parts,
which allowed it to keep on existing,
which allowed it to make more parts,
which allowed it to keep on existing,
which allowed it to make more parts,
which allowed it to keep on existing,
which allowed it to make more parts,
which allowed it to keep on existing,
which allowed it to make more parts,
which allowed it to keep on existing,
which allowed it to make more parts,
which allowed it to keep on existing,

which allowed it to make more parts,
which allowed it to keep on existing,
which allowed it to make more parts,
which allowed it to keep on existing,
which allowed it to make more parts,
which allowed it to keep on existing,
which allowed it to make more parts,
which allowed it to keep on existing,
which allowed it to make more parts,
which allowed it to keep on existing,
which allowed it to make more parts,
which allowed it to keep on existing,
which allowed it to make more parts,
which allowed it to keep on existing,
which allowed it to make more parts,
which allowed it to keep on existing,
which allowed it to make more parts,
which allowed it to keep on existing,
which allowed it to make more parts,
which allowed it to keep on existing,
which allowed it to make more parts,
which allowed it to keep on existing,
which allowed it to make more parts,
which allowed it to keep on existing,
which allowed it to make more parts,
which allowed it to keep on existing,
which allowed it to make more parts,
which allowed it to keep on existing,
which allowed it to make more parts,
which allowed it to keep on existing,

which allowed it to make more parts,
which allowed it to keep on existing,
which allowed it to make more parts,
which allowed it to keep on existing,
which allowed it to make more parts,
which allowed it to keep on existing,
which allowed it to make more parts,
which allowed it to keep on existing,
which allowed it to make more parts,
which allowed it to keep on existing,
which allowed it to make more parts,
which allowed it to keep on existing,
which allowed it to make more parts,
which allowed it to keep on existing,
which allowed it to make more parts,
which allowed it to keep on existing,
which allowed it to make more parts,
which allowed it to keep on existing,
which allowed it to make more parts,
which allowed it to keep on existing,
which allowed it to make more parts,
which allowed it to keep on existing.

Please go back and read that whole repetitious section that you just skipped. If I have any hope of communicating with you, I need you to actually read those 33 couplets, feel their repetition, struggle under the weight of the boredom and purposelessness they create. Let us use these little squibs of ink to share an experience, for last night I realized: The machine is me, and those purposeless couplets, the wheeze of my daily existence.

THERE ARE TIMES WHEN I CAN BARELY fog a mirror. My blood is thick like pulp, and it weeps through my veins. My joints are filled with sand, and sounds that had never bothered me—the fan in my computer, the hum of office lights—now set my teeth on edge, squeeze my chest. Sometimes, I go outside and stare into the blue sky for relief, but the steady racket of helicopters taking tourists over Niagara Falls, even the occasional jet flying so high it's silent, brings tears to my eyes and a nervous energy for which there is no release. All the while, my mind slowly thrums its daily mantra: God is not here. God is not here. Sometimes I can calm down and tell myself that

I'm simply lost in the jungle of my inner being. But other days, I can feel it: God really isn't here. God is only in the mountains.

What kind of God would make himself available only in certain terrains? Isn't God universal? Omnipresent? Never leaving your side? I mean, what kind of God would require us to teeter on the sides of mountains to find Him? And yet that's precisely the truth my life is revealing, and precisely the history of spirituality that Belden Lane chronicled in his book: Centuries of monks traveling great distances to inhabit deserts and mountains that fostered pure union with the Living Word. If that's so, what's left for the rest of us? How can God be that inequitable?

And what kind of spiritual awakening would lead to such a self-indulgent existence? I will never forget the words of my former pastor, Will Ingram, one day in Toronto long before I'd ever heard of Pacaya. "God is not a head game, Joe. You'll know a good spirituality by the way it changes your interactions with others." I've started to face a cold truth: Long ago, I stopped growing in compassion for my neighbor, probably about a year after my first hike up Pacaya. If anything, most people these days are obstacles to me, obstacles to the silence, obstacles to my getting back to the mountains. This path I'm on, it cannot be The Way.

THE LOBBY OF THE CORONADO HOTEL REMINDED ME of the America that the Carnegies and Rockefellers built. Gold-leaf columns rose to meet a coffered ceiling of brass and leather that spanned a dozen plush chairs, a grand piano, a stone fireplace. Subdued lighting brought a quiet to the lobby, even to the annexed cafe, that was as calming as it was rare in American public space: No TVs blaring, not a cell phone in sight. You could actually concentrate.

What brought me to St. Louis was Belden Lane, a theology professor at St. Louis University whose Solace of Fierce Landscapes was one of the few books that had really grabbed me before my self-imposed reading ban. I had emailed Belden to ask if I could meet with him for tea or coffee sometime this winter, that I'd been living a mountain spirituality for several years and had now managed to land myself in trouble. I told him I was up for the 750 mile drive, if even for an hour's time. He agreed.

At the appointed hour, a white-bearded man with an eternal smile ordered a cup of coffee in the adjacent cafe, then entered the Coronado lobby. He had a backpack instead of a briefcase. We made our introductions and small talk, and, after a few minutes, settled in.

I told him about The Crisis, how I'd developed this beautiful spirituality after Pacaya but had somehow managed to turn it into something akin to an addiction. How I'd started worshipping the mountain itself, and not because it brought any love into the world but because it gave me what I needed most: my next transcendental fix. I described the wreck I'd become living in Western New York, separated from the mountains, separated from God, my every thought focused on how to return to them, how to enter into the cosmic love I tried but failed to keep alive in meditation, how they were no longer enough, those lakeside chants, how my body seized in pain from being separated from The Mountains, the one place where I was perfectly understood and made Whole. My hands were shaking, my eyes flexed, I was somewhere between a laugh and a cry. In the end, I told him there were days I wished I'd never found that holy communion atop Pacaya.

Belden was not quick to speak. He let my long story diffuse in him, quietly searching it for a handle. Then he smiled, folded his hands, and turned the conversation inward.

"You have to have a fierce interior landscape to which you go regularly," he said. "For me, it's contemplation. That takes you to an utterly bare place inside."

He talked about his regular practice of sitting under a cherry tree at night for 15 minutes to an hour, watching the moon, the stars.

"I move into a deep place of letting go of all words, all thoughts. And that is the scariest, most compelling, most sublime place

I go," he said. The time he spends in contemplation during his everyday life, that's what brings to life the months he spends in the mountains and deserts, he explained. "It's the marriage of the inner and outer landscapes that feeds you."

That feeds you. That's what was missing from my life. Pacaya had once fed me, intensely, perfectly it'd seemed. But over the years, the tables had turned and now I was feeding it, and it left me ever and increasingly hungry. It was then that I remembered Gabor Maté's bestselling book In the Realm of Hungry Ghosts. In Buddhist thought, a hungry ghost is a pitiable creature with a vast, empty stomach and a neck too narrow to allow much food to pass. Maté draws on this imagery to present the addict as someone who relentlessly seeks something outside of himself to satisfy a void that can only be sated from within. "The aching emptiness is perpetual," writes Maté, "because the substances, objects, or pursuits we hope will soothe it are not what we really need." Belden made it sound so easy: When you're out on the land, you let its power induce a mystical moment. And when you're at home, you go inward, you visualize a barren landscape, which holds the power to push you beneath word and thought as well. Belden wasn't seeking, he was finding. And what he was finding didn't make him desperate and wild eyed, it made him grateful and well composed. The more I listened, the more I saw the hungry ghost in me.

Belden had felt what I'd felt on Pacaya. I could see it in his eyes, his manner. He knew first-hand what David Foster Wallace had meant when he spoke of being "on fire with the same force that lit the stars: love, fellowship, the mystical oneness of all things deep down." And yet he showed no signs of the desperation that had become my signature. How could that be? I mean, if he loved something that much, how could he stand to be apart from it? That was my problem. Why wasn't it his?

We talked about this for a long time without making much headway. Then it dawned on me: The way he was talking about his travels, his meditation, how it differed from the way I framed and weighted mine: "It sounds like you're a fox, Belden, whereas I'm a hedgehog." He looked puzzled, so I explained.

In 1953, the eminent Oxford philosopher Isaiah Berlin wrote an essay titled "The Hedgehog and the Fox," which, to his surprise, would become a classic. In it, Berlin argues that we can divide humans into two categories based on their thought styles. The distinction is so central to my story that I feel it warrants quoting Berlin at length:

> There is a line among the fragments of the Greek poet Archilochus which says: 'The fox knows many things, but the hedgehog knows one big thing.' Scholars have differed about the correct interpretation of these dark words, which may mean no more than that the fox, for all his cunning, is defeated by the hedgehog's one defence. But, taken figuratively, the words can be made to yield a sense in which they mark one of the deepest differences which divide writers and thinkers, and, it may be, human beings in general. For there exists a great chasm between those, on one side, who relate everything to a single central vision, one system, less or more coherent or articulate, in terms of which they understand, think and feel—a single, universal, organizing principle in terms of which alone all that they are and say has significance—and, on the other side, those who pursue many ends, often unrelated and even contradictory, connected, if at all, only in some de facto way, for some psychological or physiological cause, related by no moral or aesthetic principle. These last lead lives, perform acts and entertain ideas that are centrifugal rather than

centripetal; their thought is scattered or diffused, moving on many levels, seizing upon the essence of a vast variety of experiences and objects for what they are in themselves, without, consciously or unconsciously, seeking to fit them into, or exclude them from, any one unchanging, all-embracing, sometimes self-contradictory and incomplete, at times fanatical, unitary inner vision. The first kind of intellectual and artistic personality belongs to the hedgehogs, the second to the foxes; and without insisting on a rigid classification, we may, without too much fear of contradiction, say that, in this sense, Dante belongs to the first category, Shakespeare to the second.

An all-encompassing worldview erected on the strength and vitality of a single concept, a system of thought that would organize all the confusion and chaos of this world into a manageable, even elegant flow: That idea had captivated me, driven me, my entire life. I remember lying in a corn field as a kid looking up at the daytime moon. Invariably, the wind would blow a cornstalk into view, and I would wonder: Are the moon and the cornstalk made of the same material? Or are they fundamentally different? In high school, I got my answer in the form of the periodic table of elements, that beautiful system of matter erected on the promise of a single concept: the atom. It was a joy, an emotional relief actually, to know that all the stuff of the universe—the moon, the cornstalks, the fibers in my hair, the furnaces within distant stars, the teeth of a jaguar and the intestinal juice of a fly—that all of it could be reduced to such a finite thing as an 8"x10" chart that fit on Mrs. Larson's overhead projector in sixth period. It was simple, it was all-encompassing, that periodic table was a hedgehog's dream.

In college, I seized on the ancient Greek's insistence that in their journey through space, celestial bodies traced out circles and nothing more. When that didn't work, when the Greeks noticed a kind of back and forth motion of some of the planets against the celestial canopy that was inconsistent with circular orbits, they introduced an elaborate theory of planetary motion based on epicycles, which, in the end, were nothing more than circles upon circles. Sitting in astronomy lecture, I sympathized with those Greeks clinging to their circle, their One True Concept, as their worldview turned to sand.

Later, when studying the world's religions, I became overwhelmed by the complexities involved in even defining the word. Some religions are based on faith, others on practice. Some believe in a god of some sort, others see god as an illusion. Then a friend casually noted that all religions are unified by one thing: They are all responses to suffering. Voila. I had my One True Concept with which to move forward, my one totalizing concept upon which an effective understanding of the entirety of the world's religions—the entirety of human existence?—could be built: Until that concept was shown to be lacking and the search for the One True Concept was back on.

In graduate school, my inner hedgehog really took off when I discovered the atomic debates of the 19th and early 20th centuries, which in turn led me to a thesis on the topic and later to much of the work that would earn me tenure as a professor. The debates were as much about how scientists should think about nature as they were about nature itself, the hot issue being whether conceptual metaphors—the thinking of one thing in terms of another, the atom as a miniature solar system, for example, or electricity as water—whether these sorts of mental gymnastics merited a place in the orthodox practice of science alongside mathematics and literal expression. Metaphors were fine for teaching, all could agree, but were they a legitimate way for scientists to think about the physical world themselves?

On one side, you had the corpuscularists, led by the famed Austrian physicist Ludwig Boltzmann, who sought to explain all physical phenomena in terms of invisible bodies in motion, not unlike the billiard balls, springs, pumps, and pulleys of daily life. The corpuscularists thought the best way to do science was this: First, you draw on a conceptual metaphor or two to create a model of the thing you're studying: gases became billiard balls ricocheting off each other in a closed space, an electromagnetic field became a network of interlocking gears. Then you deduce from your conceptual model the properties it would likely exhibit based on the known laws of physics, and you compare your deduced properties to the actual findings emanating from laboratories all across Europe and the US: If the properties matched, your model—aka your scientific theory—gained factual ground; if they didn't, you would revise your concepts and try again. As you might imagine, corpuscularist thought led inevitably to an unwavering commitment to the corpuscle of all corpuscles in 19th century thinking, the atom. And I remember feeling a certain kind of nervous relief, akin to what I felt when the periodic table of elements first flashed before my eyes, when, in reading the work of John Heilbron, I came across the German physiologist Emil du Bois-Reymond, who, speaking for all corpuscularists, flatly defined the whole endeavor of science as "the action by which we reduce observations of the physical universe to the mechanics of atoms." There it was again: Order.

On the other side, you had the energeticists, who found their champion in the Baltic German chemist Wilhelm Ostwald. Rather than try to explain the physical world through imaginary contraptions, the energeticists argued, scientists should settle down to the business of accurately describing it by expressing the quantitative relationships that exist between its measurable qualities. In this way, scientists could free themselves from the speculation involved in scientific theory building, and create a ground-up science that was literal and objective, its laws irrevocable. The energeticists touted Boyle's law, which states that the volume of a gas is inversely proportional to its pressure, as a perfect example of what their program could accomplish since both the volume of a gas and its pressure are directly measurable, their reality not based on the hypothetical billiard balls or springs or sprockets found in the corpuscularists' toolbox. But Boyle's law was limited to a small subset of physical phenomena, prompting Oswald to ask: What quantity would be present in all phenomena and as direct in measurement and expression as volume or pressure? His answer was, as we might expect, energy. It was energy that connected the world "out there" to the mind "in here" because it was energy, and energy alone, that stimulated our five senses. Yes, energy, that great messenger between us and everything we could know, the one thing in nature that would never leave us. It was therefore energy, and not some imaginary collection of invisible bodies wriggling in space, that should serve as the bedrock of modern science, the starting point for all concepts and calculations if we were ever to build a truly reliable body of scientific knowledge.

I venerated those scientists. Despite their fundamental differences, they were hardcore hedgehogs, every last one of them, and the atomic debates, the best cage match in town, the corpuscularists holding up the atom as the One True Concept upon which to build a science of the universe (to my demise, I failed to recognize that they separated their science from their life), the energeticists circling the ring, firm in their resolve that energy was the true top dog. I didn't care what sorts of claims I could make in my thesis. I didn't care which side won. (The corpuscularists eventually did, thanks to Einstein.) I only wanted to wade into their ocean and stay as long as life would let me.

Such is the life of a hedgehog, moving from one concept to the next in search of the One True Concept that would pick the lock of existence. I would salivate when I thought of those tumblers falling into place and the universe in all its order and simplicity being laid bare. And from what I could see, Belden was beholden to none of it. A fox at heart, he was able to live off the breath of many concepts, many intuitions, many hints and gut feelings and insensate awareness without feeling the need to pick one as the most primary, the most fundamental, the sole cornerstone of an impeccably ordered Whole. Talking with him, I got the sense that his mental landscape was filled with streams and tributaries of past experience, all flowing in and out of each another, reinforcing each other, pliable with time. There was no lock to pick, no anxiety to quell. Whereas I needed my categories to be eternal—suffering, love, truth, mind—Belden's blew in on the wind, present about as long as they illuminated the moment. And this facile mental life, it brought him great riches. Anyone could see that.

After an hour, maybe two, I think we both felt the end of our time together drawing near. It was mid-afternoon and time to get on with the day.

"I'd like to end with a story," Belden said. It was a story that left me speechless. After he told it, I simply sat there and breathed deeply, as if I were taking a drag off the wisdom floating in the air. I knew enough not to ruin the moment by talking. Then I stood and extended my hand. Belden gave me a hug instead. We agreed to wish each other well in whatever forms our prayers took, and we departed. The story—and you have to remember, it was told by a master story-teller—was this:

A long time ago, there was a man named Isaac, son of Yekel, who lived in Krakow. Isaac was a poor man, but a good one, and he prayed nightly for the means to support his family. After a while, he started having wondrous, vivid dreams of a treasure hidden away under a fancy bridge in a town called Prague, a place he'd never heard of. The villagers thought Isaac was crazy. "Isaac," they would tell him, "it's just a dream. You can't go around listening to your dreams." But listen Isaac did. One day, he got together some bread and water and a knapsack, and set forth for this place called Prague. When he arrived days later, he was elated: The city looked just as it did in his dreams: the same spires soaring into the sky, the same cobblestone roads, the same fancy bridge. As he scaled down the bridge, a soldier captured him. "What are you doing scurrying around the bridge, Jew?" Isaac told him the truth, but the soldier just laughed. "You can't follow what you see in dreams! Why, for weeks I've been dreaming that I'd meet a man named Isaac, son of Yekel, from a village called Krakow, and under his fireplace would be a treasure. I certainly can't spend my days trying to find this man!" Isaac agreed and returned home immediately. He uprooted his fireplace and sure enough there was the treasure.

Belden had heard this story in a synagogue. "Isn't it interesting," the rabbi had noted, "that the treasure was always at home, but Isaac had to travel to Prague to find it."

There was silence. Then Belden leaned in.

"I don't want to dismiss your call to the mountains, Joe. But what you don't seem to realize is that the sacred landscape is you."

*   *   *

After St. Louis, I pointed the car north and drove to Minnesota to visit family. It was a more perilous drive than I'd expected, having run into a blizzard in Iowa City that shut down the highway and demanded that I spend the night on the University of Iowa campus. After settling into a hotel, I set out by foot to find the Dey House, home to the fabled Iowa Writers' Workshop, the first and still finest creative writing program in the country. Kurt

Vonnegut, Robert Penn Warren, Philip Roth, Wallace Stegner, John Cheever, Jane Smiley, John Irving: They'd all taught or studied there. And probably for that reason, its library served as a place of uncommon inspiration that night as I let the significance of Belden's words settle in me.

The next day on the road, things got to bothering me. I hadn't had time to talk with Belden about the curious way memory and imagery worked in me. My account of my first hike up Pacaya, which I offered in my first letter to you, which I'd offered to Belden when I asked him to coffee, it's actually a composite of two trips I took up the volcano separated by about six months. It was on that first trip with Steve in the summer of 2009 that I first slipped beneath mind and self and experienced the Great Nothingness in all its mystical oneness, and that happened before a river of lava that sprang forth near the top of the volcano and slowly oozed down its side. It wasn't until I hiked Pacaya again, in January of 2010 with two other friends, that I encountered that shimmering wall of rock that, in dismantling itself boulder by fiery boulder, presented me with the perfect imagery to express my own dismantling from the first trip. Over time, the two trips fused in my mind: The first gave me my first mystical experience, the second gave me the imagery to represent that experience to others and even to myself. It was that image of a swelling, swaying, eventually self-annihilating wall of rock that I carried with me to Nepal and to Balrum's fire, carried with me to the shores of Lake Ontario. And it's that same wall of rock that I carry with me today as I continue to learn how to unhook my spirituality from the fat spires of mountains without losing all the spiritual energy they provide. To tell the story of Pacaya with a river of lava instead of my wall of rock would be to tell someone else's story, a story that, in remaining true to a certain fact of geography, forfeits the lived truth of what it was like to be there, what it's like to live in its memory. And yet still I wondered: Is it wrong to tell my story this way? New to creative non-fiction writing, I was unsure of myself, and hoped that Belden could steady the ladder.

Nor had I found time to mention to Belden that while the desert and mountain terrains discussed in his book surely provided the conditions for mystical encounters, underwater landscapes worked as well, a fact I'd discovered on a Christmas vacation in Cancun when my girlfriend, Samantha, and I went snorkeling in submerged caverns called *cenotes*. Spying down on the limestone stalagmites that jutted up from the desolate cavern floor, I was astonished to find myself slipping beneath mind and self and entering into the mystical, my body floating on the water, silent save my breathing, the only sign of life: the few bats that fluttered overhead. I came back from that trip filled with the feeling that I had an amazing secret, almost an affair with God, an important terrain not addressed in Belden's book.

Arriving in Minnesota the next day, I stopped by my brother's house in the late afternoon and, surprisingly, found him home. We sat in the kitchen and caught up on the normal stuff. At some point, the conversation turned to my road trip, and I explained that I'd just come from coffee with Belden in St. Louis, where we talked about my possible addiction to the mountains.

"I can't get mountains off my mind," I said. "When I'm there, God, the world, me, we're all so much better. Distinctions fall away and we all become One and I feel like I'm a part of something perfect. When I'm not there, I spend all my time trying to get back. I've lost interest in my life below 8,000 feet. The wine has no taste down here."

"Have you ever had that?" I asked automatically.

A small smile drew across Scott's face.

"Yes," he said, "in combat."

A forward air controller (FAC) stationed in Germany during

Operation Desert Storm, Scott was asked to volunteer for Iraq one morning, and was on his way to the desert that afternoon. The job of the FAC is roughly this: The Army decides to strike a target by air, but it can't do it alone. So the FAC hikes out solo into the desert, the mountains, the what-have-you to establish visual contact with the target, and then, using his radio, directs the aircraft to the bullseye. After that, the idea is to get out of Dodge before what's left of the enemy finds you. In Scott's case, the aircraft were usually A-10 Warthogs, America's premier tank destroyers; the targets, hundreds of Iraqi troops marching through the sand, their tanks and armored personnel carriers in tow.

"While I wouldn't call it happiness," he said, "I had a very clear awareness and a closeness to God in combat. My physical senses were heightened. I could see, hear, smell, and feel on a different level. I could see so clearly, for example, I often didn't even wear my glasses. And it was more than just seeing clearly. It was like seeing with instant comprehension. If I needed to run to a new spot, I would just look in that direction and sort of glide or float to that position with no worry of tripping or feeling tired or winded. Like I had no physical contact with my surroundings, just mental contact. Not out of body, but more like my physical activity was controlled with very little conscious thought. All of my mind and senses were always focused on being a totally understanding part of my surroundings."

"What about the God part?" I interjected.

"When I was on a battlefield," he continued, "God was everywhere. Not many different places, but permeating everything. Maybe like a blanket and the physical world was like bits and pieces of thread within the blanket. With the God presence, I had no fear of dying. It was very clear that our lives here are a small, very small, part of an overall Something. So dying had no meaning of end or ending, just a moving on. Overall, combat was a very clear, simple, and connected scenario. In a weird way, it was holy and peaceful and maybe even happy."

After a pause, he continued. "At the time, there's no real judgment of the right or wrong of what you're doing. It was clear it was already predestined. I was there a very short period, too. I think that would change if you were there a long time, like the Vietnam veterans, as far as questioning of morality of what you were doing. In a way, I would say God was on both sides, but probably so was the devil."

I was dumbfounded. I was so used to people shaking their heads with confusion when I brought up my mountain experience that I didn't know what to say when someone related to it. Yes, his was in the context of war, but Scott's knowing nod to the mystical looked a lot more like Yuri's than I ever would have imagined.

"Do you ever try to get that feeling back?" I asked.

The short of it is no, he didn't. The war ended, he returned to the US, and life went on. But Scott did wonder if some combat veterans turn to drugs back home to try to recreate the mystical experience they'd found on the battlefield. "Maybe it's not always that they're escaping war through drugs," he said. "Maybe for some, it's their way of trying to relive that feeling of battle."

THE BELGIAN PAINTER FERNAND BERCKELAERS once imagined a kind of painting that would illustrate nothing, and in that nothingness bring us into contact with "the incommunicable kingdom of the spirit." That kingdom, I finally know something of that kingdom where form and substance simply do not apply. It must be where our development, our Becoming if not our entire Being, exists; of this, I feel sure. And therefore I am not so sure my thoughts, much less my words, so straight and brittle and here among the atoms, can excavate the sources of my recent transformation with the same precision as they could detail, for example, my time with Balrum around the fire, with Belden over coffee. I am that kid in class who receives answers too large for his questions. They slop around in my mind day and night, and spill and run down the clean edges of my orderly inquiry. I'm willing to trade some accuracy for clarity, but as one of my heroes, the German philologist Hans Blumenberg, once wrote, a preoccupation with clarity can obscure the larger mission:

> The process of cognition entails losses. To define time as what one measures with a clock seems sound and is a highly pragmatic way of avoiding disputes. But is this what we have earned since we began to ask what time is?

Yes, a compromise is necessary if we are to commit anything spiritual to ink, but this letter must do a better job of explaining the trajectory of my change than a Casio does of explaining time. When I began writing these letters, I thought they would chart out a beautiful, curved line in space, connecting the dots of my life with mathematical precision. The more I write, the more I see them as an attempt to lasso the heart of a few lived experiences.

First, there was the question of my addiction. I returned to Maté's *Hungry Ghosts*, this time studying it for answers.

To help his readers understand the inner life of an addict, Maté introduced the term salience attribution, which he defined as "the assignment of great value to a false need and the depreciation of true ones." I knew The Crisis had something to do with this, I knew my dependence on mountains was imbalanced, and not in a way that revealed a praiseworthy commitment to the divine over the mortal priorities of comfort, safety, and longevity, the way we might say Dietrich Bonhoeffer and Mother Teresa were imbalanced. No, I was just plain imbalanced, living with the kind of vertigo that comes from misplacing your basic reference points in life. But that's as far as I could take it back then, a highlight in Maté's book, a star next to the term.

Maté also claimed that addictions are "more about desire than attainment. In the addicted mode, the emotional charge is in the pursuit and the acquisition of the desired object, not in the possession and enjoyment of it." In other words, the chase is better than the catch. Turning to his own addiction to classical music, Maté confided that the rush came as he approached the music store, as he flipped through the bins of CDs, as he walked to the counter to make them his own. The adrenalin lived in the anticipation, and therefore once he'd left the store, his mind would fixate on tomorrow's purchase, tomorrow's ritual, the momentary satisfaction of today's already fading into the distance before he'd listened to a single CD. Reading his account, I winced. There had been times on Pacaya when, in the middle of enjoying the hike, the worry of not being able to return would creep up and ruin the moment. Usually it waited until I was on the flight home: I would be reflecting on what an amazing time I'd had, and worry would descend on me: What if I can't get back soon enough to keep this spirituality alive? What if there comes a day when I can't afford these trips? What if the Guatemalan government closes Pacaya to the public? That was bad enough, but when that worry would slither up the arrow of time and assail me while I was still on the mountain, I think that was probably the closest I came to addiction.

Yes, some of Maté's ideas had a familiar and unsettling ring to them, and helped me excavate the motivations that had led to The Crisis, but when he turned to the actual people, the similarities between their lives and mine ended, both on the surface and deep down.

Sharon was a woman of unstoppable vitality whose 20-something beauty had given way to the 30-something signature of a drug-sunk life: hollow cheeks, rotting teeth, a body twisted in pain. She had a habit of using dirty needles to inject her heroin, which held the door wide open for bacterial infections. The invading organisms fed on her skin, requiring her to endure skin graft after skin graft that never took. Eventually, they attacked her left knee, bone and tissue alike, leaving it chronically swollen, abscessed. Sharon was confined to a wheelchair by 33 and dead at 35 because she couldn't stay away from the dirty needles long enough to complete the two-month hospital stay required for an antibiotic treatment to take effect. In the final year of her life, doctors informed her that she was HIV positive and facing a left leg amputation from the thigh down, but it was that next fix of heroin that she met with urgency.

Then there was Ralph. It's difficult to say whether Ralph's cocaine habit had caused his ailments or merely sabotaged any hope of managing them, but the list was long, starting with hepatitis C, diabetes, an arthritic ankle, and trouble swallowing. His shaved head and Hitler mustache were no mere fashion statement. Unable to find stable emotional ground, Ralph vacillated between rarefied moments of reciting long passages of Goethe, Nietzsche, and Homer—in their original German and Greek—and rage-filled episodes when he would spit out a windstorm of anti-Semitic untruths that he tried to pass off as history. At the end of one appointment, he offered a staunch Nazi salute and "Heil Hitler!" to Maté, a Hungarian Jew who barely survived the Holocaust. Months later, laid up in a hospital bed, a sober Ralph apologized to Maté—only to return to the hot invectives and Nazi graffiti once he hit the street.

The odd man out was Dean, a top salesman for IBM who was pulling down six figures a year back when six figures really meant something, all the while shooting heroin morning and night and going at it especially hard on the weekends. Like all of Maté's clients, Dean soon started the spiral. When his wife and kids eventually left him, he blew $180,000 on cocaine in six months, then landed himself in prison for six years for drug-related crimes. But Dean turned it around: After prison, he co-founded VANDU, the Vancouver Area Network of Drug Users, a community support group for users and former users working to improve their lives. He became a well-known advocate for safe injection sites and other harm-reduction policies in the Vancouver area. He even escorted politicians through the streets of Vancouver's down-and-out side to show them what a life of drugs really looks like; and when they invited him to their side of town, he garnered their respect by giving an impassioned testimony before a Senate committee on addiction. And yet for all his activism and drive, at the time of Maté's writing, Dean was still using.

Finally, there was Celia, age 30, expectant mother. On the other side of Celia's cocaine and heroin benders were occasional threats of suicide, at least one involuntary stay in a psychiatric hospital for refusing to cooperate with firefighters during a hotel blaze, and malady after malady including broken bones and black eyes, a fungus-filled mouth, shingles, and HIV. Beating the odds, she gave birth to a healthy baby girl who was weaned from her own chemical dependency without incident. Then the odds took revenge: Through a series of court orders, Celia lost her daughter to her boyfriend, Jack, who in turn lost her to foster care. (Jack had his own demons, Child Protective Services soon discovered.) Celia dreamed of one day regaining custody of her daughter, but a dream it would remain. If the odds were right, she would never give up her cocaine.

There were others, dozens in fact, expertly detailed by Maté. But in none of them did I see my reflection. Maté's clients, they had endured lives of unimaginable suffering: Underneath the violence and prostitution and bodies vanquished of all but a pulse, under the chronic and criminal lying and cheating and stealing for drugs, were childhood years filled with torment: abuse, abandonment, rape, even torture. I certainly had nothing to compare.

And while their circumstances did vary—some enjoying healthier, more mainstream lives than others—the variations all orbited a common behavioral reality, one I found heart wrenching but ultimately one I had a hard time relating to: Maté's clients, they simply could not stop. Reading about their lives, I realized an addiction is not a relationship with the wrong kind of thing. It's the wrong kind of relationship with anything, a relationship in which the thing is in control, not you.

That was not my case with the mountains. It wasn't that I couldn't stop, it was that I didn't want to. I had equated the mountains with God, the Living Water of which Jesus spoke, the Alpha, the Omega, the Great Unnameable and Creator of All who was and is and ever shall be. Who in his right mind would want to abandon that?

No, after reading Maté's book, I realized it wasn't addiction that was suffocating me, it was something else: a conceptual problem, as if somewhere deep within me lived a syllogism that severely limited the ways I could enter into relationship with the world. And it went something like this:

Premise: God is only in the mountains.
Premise: I am not in the mountains.
Conclusion: Therefore, God is not with me.

I remember the day I first shed the language of addiction and saw this syllogism in my head. It was summer, the afternoon, I was on a run on the dirt road behind my house. When I saw that first premise, I knew it to be true; my years of travel had borne it out concretely. And yet the tide of my suffering won out that day: I had reconsidered everything else in my life, twisting and turning every thought, every detail, trying to squirm out from under the weight of The Crisis. Why not question the only assumption I had left? In my head, I have a way of dimming a proposition—literally seeing it as greyed out (maybe everybody does this?)—and considering the ripple of consequence created by its absence. I greyed out the idea that God is only in the mountains, and suddenly, surprisingly, I felt a weight had lifted. I had known or read of others who, in the midst of cognitive-behavioral therapy, had succeeded in removing a limiting belief—"I am unlovable," "I don't deserve happiness"—and had witnessed profound healing, but this was only the second time in my life I had experienced a shift so radical by simply changing something I held in my head. The first thing I noticed was how beautiful the tall grasses were, how colorful the whole landscape was: the green fields, the black earth, the sky blue and white and unending. Next I felt the constant pull to be somewhere else had been suspended. For a time, I was invigorated, I was hopeful, I was spiritually content out there on my run, centered in my own being—and without a mountain in sight. Then reality set back in—the inertia of old habits is strong—and again I was aching for the mountains. What kind of God would require us to hang off the sides of mountains to know him? The kind of God you create in your own mind: That was the unsettling thought that slowly bubbled up and swam into view as I finished my run, a grain of awareness that was as pregnant with anxiety as it was with freedom. This went on for many weeks, this mental toggling off and unfortunately back on of that first premise out on my runs. It began as a mental exercise, my pretending that God was not confined to the mountains. Over time, I began to believe it.

Why had it taken me so long to grey out that first premise? Fear. Fear owing to sloppy thinking. So fused were God and the mountains in my mind, so blended were their essences, that I couldn't distinguish between the two. To question one was to question the other, and in the midst of The Crisis the last thing

I wanted to do was upset that apple cart. At the time, I couldn't express it in words. All I knew was that I felt needles of guilt, primarily in my cheeks and forehead, whenever I looked in the direction of that first premise with anything but a smile, and that was enough, in the split-second firings of the brain, to persuade me to look under a different rock for answers. It wasn't until those summer runs, when The Crisis was really fevering through me, that I realized the mountains and God could be different, that one might be a symbol, the other the thing symbolized, and therefore that I might be able to stop worshipping the former without abandoning the latter. Necessity is indeed the mother of invention.

There were also more egotistical forces at work. Plainly put, I loved the lifestyle of a mountain hiker. I loved the clothes, the gear, all of it ratty but functional, and the challenge of fitting it all in a 40-liter pack. I loved the trip planning: the reading of Rough Guides and blogs, the scouring of websites for cheap airfare, the inoculations against obscure diseases like Japanese encephalitis and yellow fever. I loved the simplicity, the totality of it all: the fact that every paycheck, every vacation, every possession from my boots to my bug spray functioned to bring me into the rarefied air of the mystical, usually high above some exotic culture I found exhilarating. But most of all, I loved the way the mountains brought me into conversation with others back home. It's hard to talk about God, at least in my social circles, harder yet to ask folks what they think of the mystical oneness of all things. But to talk of snow-capped mountains and active volcanoes towering over hamlets and villages in far-off lands, with comments about meditation or the divine feathered in: That was entirely acceptable, even interesting to those around me, and so I found my place in the social world. Over the years, I think I came to believe, on some silent level, that overturning that first premise would mean I would have to give up my identity as a mountain hiker. And without that, what would my life look like? And who would I be?

As the mountains lost their hold on my mind that summer, I found myself asking, at times in desperation: Now what? What single concept can take the place of the mountains, can stand at the top of the pyramid of consciousness and sire all the subordinate concepts that would be important in one's life? I would see a river and think flow, maybe that's the cardinal concept upon which to build a life. Or change. Or currents. I would watch a documentary on salmon swimming upstream and think struggle, maybe that's it. Or purpose. Or determination. Or suffering. I would read a book, like John Dewey on education, and think experience, or see an inspirational quote, like Richard Bach's "What the caterpillar calls the end of the world, the master calls a butterfly," and think transformation. I would think God or love, but rule them out because they were too intangible and too common; I would think breath or laughter, but rule them out because they were too concrete and obscure. Week after week, run after run, the search continued, independent of my will, independent of me, my body in motion, my spiritual self paralyzed, until it all came to a sudden halt when voila, a twist of the kaleidoscope: I realized that whatever monolithic concept I chose—peace, prayer, change, struggle, beauty—it would lead to the same kind of obsession I'd had with the mountains. To think really hard so you don't have to think anymore, that had been my hedgehog dream. To discover a periodic table of my own, but one that applied to life. I suppose I just wanted to feel safe, the ground no longer capable of shifting beneath me. But the ground continued to shift, as it tends to do in life, and all that stayed the same was my mind, which over time became brittle, ossified, unable to keep up with the march of progress in one's life.

I thought of a conversation I'd had with a friend back in Minneapolis. I'd told him I needed my concepts to line up perfectly, as they do in an organizational chart, the One True Concept up top, the rest on subordinate rungs. Shawn said he saw his concepts as overlapping circles that could move around in their relation to one another. At the time, I was astonished. How could we understand each other, relate to each other so well, appreciate many of the same things in life when we experienced reality so differently? I mean, he let his concepts float around and overlap for God's sake, change their relation, their relative importance to each other. How could such mental hooliganism produce such an articulate person, so intelligent and rigorous and clear in perspective in the midst of life's mess? And yet the more I ran the dirt road that summer, the more I saw the resemblance between Shawn's circles and the streams and tributaries that seemed to populate Belden's mind—and I began to appreciate the mental dexterity this alien way of thinking afforded them both. Shawn and Belden, they seemed capable of bringing the right conceptual light to the moment, and with that came a fluidity to their thinking, a bounce and flow. They were flexible thinkers, whereas my mind had become staid and brittle, and in that flexibility, I could see there was wisdom.

The brick through the window came when Samantha and I attended a reading by Richard Blanco, a poet plucked from obscurity when the White House tapped him to write and deliver a new poem on the occasion of President Obama's second inauguration. Blanco is a master orator. He had his audience laughing out loud, shoulders bouncing, at the usually refined Kleinhans Music Hall the night we saw him in Buffalo, and I laughed too until he read these words:

We're Not Going to Malta . . . *because the winds are too strong,* our captain announces, his voice like an oracle coming through the loudspeakers in every lounge and hall, as if the ship itself were speaking. We're not going to Malta—*an enchanting island country fifty miles from Sicily,* according to the brochure of the tour we're not taking. But what if we *did go to Malta? What if, as we are escorted on foot through the walled "Silent City" of Mdina,* the walls begin speaking to me; and after we *stop a few minutes to admire the impressive architecture,* I feel Malta could be *the* place for me. What if, as we *stroll the bastions to admire the panoramic harbor and stunning countryside,* I dream of buying a little Maltese farm, raising Maltese horses in the green Maltese hills. What if, after we *see the cathedral in Mosta saved by a miracle,* I believe that Malta itself is a miracle; and before I'm *transported back to the pier with a complimentary beverage,* I'm struck with Malta fever, discover I am very Maltese indeed, and decide I must return to Malta, learn to speak Maltese with an English (or Spanish) accent, work as a Maltese professor of English at the University of Malta, and teach a course on The Maltese Falcon. Or, what if when *we stop at a factory to shop for famous Malteseware,* I discover that making Maltese crosses is my true passion. Yes, I'd get a Maltese cat and a Maltese dog, make Maltese friends, drink Malted milk, join the Knights of Malta, and be happy for the rest of my *Maltesian* life. But we're not going to Malta. Malta is drifting past us, or we are drifting past it—an amorphous hump of green and brown bobbing in the portholes with the horizon as the ship heaves over whitecaps wisping into rainbows for a moment, then dissolving back into the sea.

It was then that I realized just how debilitating my hedgehog thinking had become, and how, more than anything else, it was this style of thinking, so obsessive and singular, so perfectly lampooned by Blanco's poem, that had led me into the jaws of my crisis. It wasn't that the One True Concept was eluding me;

it was that the assumption that there was a One True Concept was misguided from the start. Early 20th century physicists may have had their atom, that top dog concept that unified everything in their field, but there is no atom when it comes to living. That, I learned after many days and nights of quiet suffering. Shawn's overlapping circles, Belden's streams and tributaries: They became the tendrils of a new kind of consciousness that grew in my imagination and soon intertwined and formed the next branch for me to swing for. It's a little embarrassing, but if I'm honest, I have to say that this new way of thinking reminded me of Bruce Lee's "Be Like Water" interview, where Lee famously says:

> Empty your mind.
> Be formless.
> Shapeless.
> Like water.
> Now you put water into a cup, it becomes the cup.
> You put water into a bottle, it becomes the bottle.
> You put it in a tea pot, it becomes the tea pot.
> Water can flow, or it can crash.
> Be water, my friend.

It was easier than I thought, the change from hedgehog to fox, and it began with the image of a broken mirror. When I would catch myself obsessing over a single concept the way Blanco prized Malta, be it *mountains* or *transformation* or *love*, I would see it written on a single pane of glass in my mind's eye. I would then crack it with a hammer, fracturing the pane into three, five, maybe eight pieces—each piece worthy in its own right, reflecting an important part of reality not seen in the original. It was a case of the sum of the parts becoming greater than the whole, the way your vision improves when you go from looking at something out of one eye to both, that single concept I'd started with now occupying just one of the many shards lying there in my mind. And as for the blank shards, my intuition would quickly find names to write on them, concepts that had long been suppressed by my inner hedgehog, sometimes for years. By mid-winter, it was no longer a matter of agonizing over whether the Father, Son, or Holy Spirit was the One True Concept; whether I was a writer, a Christian, or a Buddhist first; whether the mountains, deserts, or seas were the holiest landscape; whether discursive or nondiscursive mind offered the finest form of prayer; whether the contemplative or active life was better; whether mathematics or natural languages like English and French were the true bedrock of scientific thought; whether circles were more fundamental than squares. It was no longer a matter of picking the One True Concept, shoehorning the rest into logical slots beneath it, and jettisoning the ones that didn't fit, the way I'd jettisoned so many things in my life: my interest in computer programming because it didn't fit under the rubric of Writer; anger or frustration because it didn't seem to accord with In All Things Love; prairies, plains, seascapes, and cities because they weren't The Mountains. Now, every concept had its own shard of mental glass, and to my surprise, they intermingled and enriched each other rather than try to drown each other in the stream of my consciousness (as many were known to do back in the hedgehog days). By the new year, they produced something in me that I can only describe as a concert of awareness, probably because I let myself consider things from multiple perspectives at the same time, notes upon notes creating harmonies I never knew existed, the kind of thing that's just not possible when you spend your whole life plinking away at just one key. Life's moments began to add to each other, even the difficult ones. My mood elevated and stabilized, the merciless organizational chart I'd lived with for so many years and which had dimmed everything I'd experienced in the world, gone. And so I came to live by a constellation of concepts, ever changing, ever generated by the nexus of the moment and me and hopefully the Spirit and the smashing of those single panes of glass, and in so doing, I found my way into thinking like a fox.

Then there was Isaac, son of Yekel. Belden's story of the man who had to travel to Prague to realize the treasure was always at home, that story stayed with me all winter, all summer, and only in the fall did I realize it had seeped into my bones. On a backpacking trip in Guatemala that year with Samantha (who can sleep in like a rock star), I found myself walking alone one morning outside a tiny village called El Hato, roosters crowing, a single mountain peak towering over the tree line. It was our final day in the country, in a few hours we would be sitting despondently in a food court in the airport, so I just stared at the mountain as if to say goodbye, a ritual I'd started instinctively after Pacaya. It was my way of taking a piece of the mountain home with me, burying its special power in my heart and memory in the hopes it would get me through until the next encounter, building that inner landscape Belden had talked about. But that morning, it was different. I realized that what I'd thought was a quality of the mountains had all along been a quality of me, a quality of all of us, that I was taking home not what the mountains had given me but what they had awakened in me, what had been there all the while, this sleeping Spirit. Years earlier, Pacaya had torn something open in me, allowing new life to breathe, but somewhere along the way, I set my sights on the mountains rather than the new life. Probably because it seemed more adventurous, probably because it was more socially appropriate, probably because I identified with tropical landscapes more than I identified with my own inner life. Whatever the reason, I had mistaken the tool for the task, and in so doing, entered into many years of suffering, a Hungry

Ghost forever filling up on the wrong thing. I had misunderstood Belden. He hadn't meant that I should start visualizing the mountains so I could lean on their power to keep me afloat. No, I think he was encouraging me to use the image of the mountains—or anything else for that matter—to find what he called that "utterly bare place inside," the place where the Spirit that is me that is all of us that is God roams free of the chains of language. There on the horizon, I could see it: not only the mystical mountain, but also the mystical me. And in that vision, I stepped into a new incarnation of myself.

"**WORDS,** WROTE WILLIAM JOHNSTON, "are like a finger pointing to the moon. Cling to the finger and you'll never see the moon." This ancient aphorism is often used to illuminate the difference between symbols of God and God itself, and in so doing, to remind us not to let our representations eclipse reality. (If you're bothered by my use of "itself," ask yourself why. Is it God or your mental image of God that doesn't reconcile with the term?) When we worship a sacred scripture rather than the divine reality the scripture points to, when a religious painting becomes more important than the thing painted, when our own mental image of God is understood as God itself, I believe we are mistaking the finger for the moon. We clutch the signifier because it is amenable to the mind, forget the signified because it is not, and voila, slip into a life of fetish. This common conflation is the basis for the famous Buddhist saying, "If you meet the Buddha, kill him." What you are seeing is an image, a representation of the Buddha, not the elusive truth the Buddha taught.

What I failed to see for so many years is that mystical experiences are also fingers pointing to the moon. Fingers closer to the moon, maybe fingers massaging the moon, but fingers nonetheless. A mystical experience of God is not the same thing as God anymore than jumping into a swimming pool is the same thing as the swimming pool. Or, to use a less obvious example, loving making love to a certain someone isn't the same thing as loving that someone. And if you've fallen for that mistake in the past, you know all too well how abysmally those relationships usually unfold outside the bedroom. My friend Robert, a Harvard trained theologian whose mind is ever amazing me, captured the sentiment with his usual clarity over drinks one night. "God is bigger than any experience of God," he said, and with that, he said it all.

A T THE CENTER OF THE FRIENDSHIP VILLAGE, an orphanage in Hanoi where Samantha and I volunteered last year and for which I've been fundraising ever since, you'll find a soccer field, paved and painted, encircled by tall elm and palm trees, themselves surrounded by a half-dozen residential villas modelled in the French tradition, a sight totally incongruous to the battered Vietnamese neighborhood of Van Canh that lay just beyond the gates.

I sat on a park bench overlooking the soccer field one morning last April as a chorus of insects called the sun out of hiding. A frog happened across the pavement, three hops then rest, three hops then rest, and I thought of the journey each of us is on. The frog cut a path far more direct and confident than my own circuitous route, which has taken me from Guatemala to St. Louis by way of the Himalayas, from ecstasy to despair to the balance I feel today in a life directed by a phrase I reflect on daily: *via contemplativa, via activa.*

What I first found on Pacaya and later on the shores of Lake Ontario, I now find most often while running. Jogging actually, a slow, steady pace just faster than a walk, which I usually maintain for an hour or two. Whereas in Zen meditation, one practices "just sitting," I suppose you could say I practice "just running." I pay no attention to time or distance. I try to leave the expectation of comfort behind. It's not a goal-driven run, not a run into the future, but a witnessing of the moving present. One foot in front of the other. That is all.

It's in running that I come closest to what today goes by the name of mindfulness. When I get bored, I simply notice that boredom. *This is what boredom feels like. Is it a good reason to stop running? No.* When my body starts to revolt, I simply try to witness it. *This is what knee pain feels like. Is it a good reason to stop running? No.* Sometimes the sky intervenes. *This is what it feels like to run in the rain. This is what it feels like to be cold and running. This is me running with a runny nose. Are these good reasons to stop? No.*

Over time, I think once it realizes it's lost its power over me, my mind stops throwing up all the excuses it can think of to get me to stop running. It quiets. And on the other side of the boredom and the excuses and the pain, I sometimes find my old friend waiting for me, the Great Unnameable. It's rarely as powerful as that first time on Pacaya, but in at least one way, it's more edifying: It's no longer a head game for me, this slipping beneath language and self. It's no longer a thing to maximize, to optimize, to poke and see how it responds. No, the other side of silence is a place where I enter into unmediated relationship with God. There's no controlling it. There's only being open to it, grateful when it happens, faithful when it doesn't. And when I'm willing to see it that way, it feeds me deeply, cares for me, and in so doing, gives me the motivation to care for others.

The frog made it across the pavement just in time. A minute later, a Vietnamese girl swept its path with a broom made from Jurassic-sized palm fronds as some kids made their way down from the villas to play soccer before breakfast. A few had pronounced limps, others scoliosis, one was in his 20s but confined to the body of an eight year old. They live with a variety of maladies, these "invisible children" of Vietnam, from obscure cancers to pronounced neurological disorders to severe mental retardation and blindness. But they are all united, hundreds of thousands across the country, by the fact that their disability was caused by Agent Orange, a deadly defoliant dropped on Vietnam's jungles by the American military decades before they were born.

For some of the kids, their disability was encoded in their genes, an unfortunate family inheritance from grandparents and great-grandparents who were among the three million Vietnamese soldiers and civilians directly exposed to Agent Orange during the war. Others first encountered their disability in the womb, still others in baby food or their mother's breast milk since dioxin, the active ingredient in Agent Orange, is still present in the ground water and soil of much of Central Vietnam today.

According to Michael Martin, an Asian affairs analyst employed by the US federal government, a recent study of the soil from the Da Nang airbase found dioxin toxicity levels 365 times the international safe limit of 1 part per billion; the soil from the Bien Hoa airbase registered a staggering 1,000 parts per billion. Martin also cited a study of blood samples from Da Nang residents that found dioxin levels 100 times the international safe limit; elevated dioxin levels were also found in the blood samples of Bien Hoa residents. And while Da Nang and Bien Hoa are among the worst of Vietnam's dioxin hotspots, that does not mean the rest of the country is safe. In all, Martin estimates that three million of the 90 million people currently living in Vietnam suffer from a dioxin-caused disease or disability, about the same number of people who were directly exposed to Agent Orange during the war. That's how indestructible the dioxin molecule is.

It was only last summer that Samantha and I first visited the Friendship Village. We'd decided to go backpacking in Vietnam, and Samantha had suggested that we spend some time volunteering. She ran across the Friendship Village on the web one day, struck up an email conversation with them, and soon we were booked for a week's stay. We spent our days weeding the garden and helping the kids in classes ranging from hygiene to cooking, and on some of the nights, we watched them play soccer under the lights. It was on one of those nights that I shared that very same park bench with three veterans, likely from different sides of the war, who were staying at the Village for a one-month wellness retreat. They spoke softly, these former foes, fingering their cigarettes as if the slightest pressure would snap them, as a herd of kids chased a hard, plastic ball from goal to goal. It was then that I saw the magic of the Village, what its founder, an American veteran named George Mizo, had in mind when he envisioned a center for healing that would also serve as an international symbol of hope and reconciliation.

I do what I can for these kids, which so far has amounted to volunteering at the Village, fundraising back home, serving on the board of the US arm of the Village, and attending the biennial board of directors meeting, which was what brought me to Hanoi in April. For three days, board members from around the world—Germany, Japan, France, and the US—met with Village administrators and government officials to hammer out a new memorandum of agreement that would shape the strategic direction of the Village for the next two years. After dinner one night, several of us wandered down to The Romantic Cafe, an eccentric candlelit bar in Van Canh where "Beer, please" gets a milk crate of Vietnam's finest pale lager dropped on the floor next to your table. It was there that I got to know my colleagues. The youngest were in their 60s, one was pushing 80, all were effusive in personality and rich in life stories. There was talk of politics and art and mountaineering and love. There was singing and enthusiastic applause. (One of the Frenchmen had a velvet voice and a penchant for early jazz.) And, in more somber moments, there was talk of the war. All had been there, all had come back to serve these kids.

It was at The Romantic Cafe that night that I realized my role in the effort. I represent the younger generation, the 40-something Americans who, with no memory of the war, will have to pick up the baton that these veterans are laying down if there is to be continued American-Vietnamese cooperation in responding to the legacy of war: in responding to the unexploded ordnance that litters the countryside, maiming or killing hundreds of Vietnamese farmers each year; in responding to the debilitating effects of Agent Orange on generation after generation of Vietnamese children. A sadness came over me that night as I reflected on the board of directors meeting, on the fact that almost no one there would be active in ten years. The time of transition is upon us, and I wondered then as I wonder now, who among us will find it in their hearts to step up and inherit this work, to continue what these veterans have sustained for the better part of their lives?

Back in my room, I zipped into my mosquito netting, put in my earplugs, and slipped out the back door of my mind. It felt like a descent this time, marked by a few moments of shaking as I freed myself from my net of thoughts. There, for an instant, was the universe reconstituting itself moment by moment, reminding me of the static that used to come over the TV after midnight when I was a kid. I thought of Pacaya, the Friendship Village kids, Samantha back home, then geometric images and flowing water and smoke. Then I thought no more, and entered into a mystery so vast I didn't know where the universe ended and my mind began.

The next day, with the board meeting behind us, Don and I shared a cab into downtown Hanoi for lunch. A seasoned peace activist with a heart for Vietnam, Don took me under his wing when I arrived at the Village, showing me the organizational ropes and introducing me to the right people, NGO leaders from across the country who attended the biennial meeting as guests of the Village director. A young man of 20 in the war, Don actually spent some of his tour unloading barrels of Agent Orange shipped in from the US. His volunteer work at the Friendship Village represents a life having come full circle, and in this man, I found much to admire.

It was Don who went out of his way to set up a meeting for me with Chuck Searcy, an intelligence officer stationed in Saigon during the war who saw first-hand how the US government was falsely spinning the conflict for Americans back home. Chuck returned to Vietnam in the 1990s, and in 2001 co-founded one of the country's most successful bomb, landmine, and grenade disposal organizations, Project RENEW. While the organization currently serves Quang Tri province, it is poised to become the national model for munitions cleanup in Vietnam. It was from Chuck that I learned that more bombs were dropped on Vietnam during the war than all the bombs dropped on Europe during World War II; he estimated that 10% failed to detonate on impact, leaving today's Vietnam with about one million tons of unexploded ordnance waiting in the countryside for unsuspecting farmers and their children.

Over lunch in Hanoi, Don and I skirted the heavy issues and joked and covered the usual topics like old friends: women, surfing, food, and Hanoi. At the same time, I couldn't help but reflect on Don, the man: Here's a guy who splits his time between Oregon and a beach apartment on Vietnam's central coast, a guy who feels more culture shock returning to the US than he does in the land of his former foes. Here's a retiree doing anything but retiring, approaching 70 and still spending his days fundraising and writing for the cause, serving some of the most socially marginalized people in the world. And inspiring me along the way. Back on the NU campus, a few motivated students and I had raised $1985 for the Village, which administrators used to restore their organic garden. (You can imagine how important organic food is to a community of people disabled by an herbicide.) I mentioned to Don that I was now planning a biennial "Legacy of War" trip to Vietnam for NU students, which would include a tour of Chuck Searcy's Project RENEW, a volunteer stay at the Friendship Village, and some silent hiking in the mountains a few hundred miles to the north. Don, of course, enthusiastically offered to help with the planning if I needed it. We ended our lunch on a high note with talk of the future, and went our separate ways, Don back to his beach apartment, me to the night train to the Chinese border.

The contemplative, the active: To breathe, finally to breathe using both my lungs. Amen.

B I B L I O G R A P H Y

Aristotle. *The Metaphysics*. New York: Penguin, 1999.

Augustine, St. *The Confessions*. New York: Penguin, 1961.

Basho, Matsuo. *A Zen Wave: Basho's Haiku and Zen*. Berkeley, CA: Counterpoint, 2003.

Berckelaers, Fernand, in Lispector, Clarice. *Agua Viva*. New York: New Directions, 2012.

Berlin, Isaiah. *The Hedgehog and the Fox*. Lanham, MD: Ivan R. Dee/Rowman and Littlefield, 1993.

Blanco, Richard. *Directions to the Beach of the Dead*. Tucson: University of Arizona Press, 2005.

Blumenberg, Hans. *Shipwreck with Spectator*. Cambridge, MA: MIT Press, 1996.

Heilbron, John Lewis. *A History of the Problem of Atomic Structure from the Discovery of the Electron to the Beginning of Quantum Mechanics*. PhD Dissertation, 1964, University of California, Berkeley: UMI 65-3004.

James, William. *The Varieties of Religious Experience*. New York: Penguin, 1982.

Johnston, William. *Christian Zen.* Bronx, NY: Fordham UP, 1997.

Lane, Belden. *The Solace of Fierce Landscapes.* New York: Oxford UP, 2007.

Lee, Bruce. "The Lost Interview." Online video clip. YouTube. YouTube, 30 May 2014. Web. 19 May 2015.

Martin, Michael. *Vietnamese Victims of Agent Orange and US-Vietnam Relations.* Report No. RL34761. Washington, DC: Congressional Research Service, 2012.

Maté, Gabor. *In the Realm of Hungry Ghosts.* Berkeley, CA: North Atlantic Books, 2010.

Twain, Mark. *Life on the Mississippi.* New York: Dover, 2000.

Joseph Little is an associate professor of English at Niagara University, where he directs the first-year writing program and teaches courses in science writing, travel writing, and writing and well-being. He lives in Western New York with his wife, Samantha, and their 11-year-old puppy, Sister.

HOMEBOUND PUBLICATIONS

Ensuring that the mainstream isn't the only stream.

At Homebound Publications, we publish books written by independent voices for independent minds. Our books focus on a return to simplicity and balance, connection to the earth and each other, and the search for meaning and authenticity. Founded in 2011, Homebound Publications is one of the rising independent publishers in the country. Collectively through our imprints, we publish between fifteen to twenty offerings each year. Our authors have received dozens of awards, including: Foreword Review Book of the Year, Nautilus Book Award, Benjamin Franklin Book Awards, and Saltire Literary Awards. Highly-respected among bookstores, readers and authors alike, Homebound Publications has a proven devotion to quality, originality and integrity.

We are a small press with big ideas. As an independent publisher we strive to ensure that the mainstream is not the only stream. It is our intention at Homebound Publications to preserve contemplative storytelling. We publish full-length introspective works of creative non-fiction as well as essay collections, travel writing, poetry, and novels. In all our titles, our intention is to introduce new perspectives that will directly aid humankind in the trials we face at present as a global village.

WWW.HOMEBOUNDPUBLICATIONS.COM